2/7/91- Beckham's

William L. Crowe Jr.

ENGLAND,

THE UNITED STATES,

AND

THE SOUTHERN CONFEDERACY.

BY

F. W. SARGENT, M.D.

OF PHILADELPHIA.

SECOND EDITION,

REVISED AND AMENDED.

" American Slavery is the worst that ever saw the sun, it is the sum of all villanies."—JOHN WESLEY.

" Slavery is the natural and moral condition of the negro. Our new Government is the first in the history of the world based upon this great physical, philosophical, and moral truth."
—A. H. STEPHENS, *Vice-President of the Southern Confederacy.*

NEGRO UNIVERSITIES PRESS
NEW YORK

Originally published in 1864
by Hamilton, Adams and Co., London

Reprinted from a copy in the collections
of the Brooklyn Public Library

Reprinted 1969 by
Negro Universities Press
A Division of Greenwood Press, Inc.
New York

SBN 8371-2768-8

PRINTED IN UNITED STATES OF AMERICA

TO MY COUNTRY!

In freta dum fluvii current, dum montibus umbræ
Lustrabunt convexa, polus dum sidera pascet,
Semper honos, nomenque tuum, laudesque manebunt,
Quæ me cumque vocant terræ.

Æneid, lib. I.

PREFACE.

In preparing the following pages for publication, the author has been animated by the sincere desire and hope of contributing to lessen the ill-feeling which exists in Great Britain against the United States. He believes that this will be best accomplished by exhibiting important facts concerning the causes of, and the issues involved in, the American Civil War, and concerning the nature and effects of Slavery at the South, drawn chiefly from Southern authorities and from official documents. He asks for a candid reading of his Pamphlet.

Nice, *May* 1, 1864.

TABLE OF CONTENTS.

ERRATA.

Page 29, line 5,—for *one-third*, read *one-fourth.*
,, 123, line 22,—for *adverse*, read *averse.*

ENGLAND, THE UNITED STATES, AND THE SOUTHERN CONFEDERACY.

INTRODUCTION.

In all its aspects the American civil war is one of the most remarkable dramas the world has ever witnessed. Its theatre is a continent; its actors are thirty millions of people; its spectators are all the nations of the earth; upon its issue depend the fate of an oppressed race, the future of the mightiest republic of modern times, and the advancement or the retrogression of Christian civilization over a large portion of the globe.

This mighty contest is regarded by Englishmen and by loyal Americans from very different points of view. In England, while some of all classes have comprehended from the first the true nature of the struggle, others have considered it a mere war for political supremacy or independence; others, again, have seen in it nothing more than a violent disturber of British commercial and industrial interests; and a fourth and most influential class has concerned itself solely in determining how far the war might be made to benefit Great Britain, at the expense of the United States.

To us, on the other hand, the strife involves results far more momentous than mere individual interests or sufferings. Our national existence and the very principles of our form of government are at stake; unimportant or worthless, as these may be to Englishmen, to us they are priceless as his household gods to the old Greek.

We are sometimes taunted with considering an extensive

national domain as synonymous with national greatness. We refute the charge by showing what our institutions have accomplished for us, beyond mere material development. Under their influence our population has increased from three millions to thirty millions, within the recollection of men now living. They have covered the land (that part of it, at least, where they have had full sway) with schools so numerous that England is put to shame; with churches providing accommodation for the people greater, comparatively, than the city of London; with benevolent establishments of all sorts, so liberally administered that England has done us the honour to imitate them. Under their auspices science, literature, the æsthetic and mechanical arts have been so well cultivated that, all things considered, America will bear a favourable comparison with any other country.

Nor have Americans alone benefited by the institutions of America. She has fed the hungry, she has sheltered the stranger, she has clothed the naked, and ministered to the desolate of every nation under heaven. Millions of British subjects who have been thrown off from their own country, as though they had been "unclean" things, have come to America, and America has received them as her own children; she has taken outcast humanity "by the four corners," as in the strange vision of the apostle, and welcomed it to recognition. And wheresoever in all the world money and self-devotion are needed for benevolent and religious operations, America contributes her full share, and Americans are there to aid the good work.

For all these reasons we are proud of our country and our institutions, and we think them worth fighting for.

The object of the following pages is, to exhibit the true nature of the war now raging in the United States, and the issues involved in it. Let us first examine, as briefly as possible,

THE ALLEGED AND REAL MOTIVES OF SECESSION.

It is maintained by many in England that the rupture of the Union is but a natural consequence of the diversity of origin, character, and interests of the people inhabiting the two sections respectively.

Whatever may be the differences in these respects between the people of the Northern and Southern States, they have never produced any discordance of action, excepting when the question of slavery has been involved. We have waged war together against other nations (and against our common parent, when colonial idiosyncrasies were more strongly marked than they have been since); Northern ingenuity, enterprise, and capital have been freely lent to, and freely borrowed by, the South; Southerners have come to the North for education, enjoyment, and health; more than half a million natives of the South were permanent residents at the North, previous to the war; and all the elegancies and comforts of Southern homes are of Northern, when not of European, origin.

On the other hand, the population of the Free States is infinitely more heterogeneous, as every one knows, than that of the Slave States; yet this leads to no civil conflicts there. So far from it, the Northern population, diverse as it is, has united with unexampled accord to oppose this rebellion. No one can pretend, moreover, that the elements of the population in the United States are a whit more dissimilar or antagonistic than the Irish, Welsh, Scotch, and English of "the United Kingdom," to say nothing of the foreign subjects of Great Britain.

But we have on this point most weighty testimony from one of the most eminent journalists of the South, a chosen representative of South Carolina at the conventions of other Slave States. This gentleman, in discussing "*the Philosophy of Secession,*" says:—

"*The South is now in the process of forming a Slave Republic.* This, perhaps, is not generally admitted. There are many contented to believe that the South, as a geographical section, is in mere assertion of its independence. This, I fear, is an inadequate conception of the controversy. The contest is not between the North and South as geographical sections, for between such sections merely there can be no contest; nor between the people of the North and the people of the South, for our relations have been pleasant, and on neutral grounds there is still nothing to estrange us. . . . The real contest is between the two forms of society which have become established—the one at the North, the other at the South. . . . The one is a society composed of one race; the other, of two races. The one is bound together but by the two great social relations of husband and wife, and parent and child; the other by the three relations of husband and wife, and parent and child, and master and slave. The one embodies in its political structure the principle that equality is the right of man; the other, that it is the right of equals only. . . . Such, then, being the nature of the contest, *this Union has been disrupted in the effort of slave society to emancipate itself; and the momentous question now being determined is, shall that effort be successful?*"[1] &c.

It has been affirmed, and nowhere more generally and more persistently than in England, that the Southern States have taken up arms against the Federal Government in exercise of their *right* to throw off a supremacy which had become *prejudicial* to them.

The right of a people to revolt against an unjust and oppressive Government we all admit; both England and the United States owe their present liberties to its exercise. But throughout the Western Republic there has been no legalised oppression, no systematic denial of rights, save where in the Southern States four millions of human beings have been held in slavery. To prove that the South has not only not been subjected to any oppression, and has had no grievance to complain of, but that it has really governed the whole country from its national independence to the accession of Mr. Lincoln to the Presidency, we have the most unimpeachable testimony. In 1861, a convention was held in Georgia to determine whether that State should separate from the Union, in consequence of the election of Mr. Lincoln. Amongst those who opposed this step was Mr. Stephens, the actual Vice-President of the Southern Confederacy. We make the following extracts from his most remarkable speech on that occasion:—

"Pause, I entreat you, and consider what reasons you can give for this step (the secession of Georgia) which will even satisfy yourselves in calmer moments—what reasons you can give to your fellow-sufferers in the calamity that it will bring upon us! What reasons can you give to the nations of the earth to justify it? They will be the calm and deliberate judges in the case; and what cause, or what one overt act, can you name on which to rest the plea of justification? What right has the North assailed? What interest of the South has been invaded? What justice has been denied? What claim founded on justice and right has been withheld? Can any of you to-day name one governmental act of wrong, deliberately and purposely done by the Government at Washington, of which the South has a right to complain? I challenge the answer. . . . When we of the South demanded the slave-trade, or the importation of Africans for the cultivation of our lands, did not the North yield the right for twenty years? When we asked a three-fifths representation in Congress for our slaves, was it not granted? When we demanded the

[1] "The Philosophy of Secession," by the Hon. L. W. Spratt, of Charleston; reprinted in Professor Cairnes' work on "The Slave Power," pp. 392–397.

return of any fugitive from justice, or the recovery of persons owing labour or allegiance, was it not incorporated in the Constitution, and again ratified and strengthened by the Fugitive Slave Law of 1850?

"But, do you reply that, in many instances, the North has violated this compact, and been unfaithful to this engagement? Individuals and local communities may have done so, but not by the sanction of Government, for that has always been true to Southern interests. . .

"But again, gentlemen, what have we to gain by this proposed change of our relation to the general Government? We have always had the control of it, and can still control it, if we remain under it and are as united as we have been. We have had a majority of the Presidents chosen from the South, as well as the control and management of most of those elected from the North. We have had sixty years of Presidents, the North but twenty-four; thus we have controlled the Executive Department. So of the judges of the Supreme Court, eighteen have come from the South, only eleven from the North; although nearly four-fifths of the judicial business has arisen in the Free States, yet a majority of the Court has always been from the South. This we have required so as to guard against any interpretation of the Constitution unfavourable to ourselves. In like manner we have been equally watchful over our interests in the legislative branch of Government. Of the presiding Presidents (*pro tempore*) of the Senate, we have had twenty-four to their eleven. We have had twenty-three Speakers of the House of Representatives, and they twelve. Thus, while the North, from its greater population, has furnished the majority of the Representatives, we have generally secured the Speaker, because he, to a great extent, shapes and controls the legislation of the country. Nor have we had less influence in every other department of the general Government. We have provided fourteen Attorney-Generals; the North but five. We have had eighty-six Foreign Ministers; they but fifty-four. Thus, while three-fourths of the business which demands diplomatic agents abroad is clearly from the Free States, from their greater commercial interests, we have had, nevertheless, the principal Embassies, so as to secure the markets of the world on the best possible terms for our cotton, tobacco, and sugar. We have had a vast majority of the higher offices of both army and navy, while a larger proportion of the soldiers and sailors have been drawn from the North. . . .

"Again, look at another item, and one in which, be assured, we have a great and vital interest; it is that of the revenue, or the means of supporting the Government. From official documents we learn that a fraction over three-fourths of the revenue collected has uniformly been raised at the North. . . ."

Of the General Government, Mr. Stephens spoke in these terms:—

"It is the best and freest Government—the most equal in the rights it accords, the most just in its decisions, the most lenient in its measures, and the most inspiring in its principles to elevate the human race—that the sun of heaven ever shone upon. Now, for you to attempt to overthrow such a Government as this, under which we have lived for more than three-quarters of a century—under which we have gained our wealth, our standing as a nation, our domestic safety while the elements of peril are around us, with peace and tranquillity accompanied by unbounded prosperity, and rights unassailed—is the height of madness, folly, and wickedness, to which I can neither lend my sanction nor my vote."

Within a few months from the delivery of this speech, its author was elected Vice-President of the Southern Confederacy.

The *Border Slave States,*[1] in a convention held in June 1861, made the following declaration concerning the seceding States, which is in strict accordance with the opinion of Vice-President Stephens :—

"The acts of these States find no warrant in any known principle of our Government, and no justification in the facts existing, when they seceded. . . . We ask no concession of new or additional rights. We do not fear any immediate encroachment upon our rights as Slave States. . . . The States which have seceded have abandoned the best Government in the world without any good or sufficient cause."

The Southern rebellion, has, therefore, no claim to favourable consideration, on the plea of its being a *resistance to oppression,* least of all from England and Englishmen, whose dependencies, not always paternally governed, are scattered over every quarter of the globe.

The right which the Southern States claimed, and by which their rebellion is sought to be justified, is not "the right of revolution." It is the right to secede without opposition from beneath the supremacy of the Federal Constitution, when, in the judgment of a portion of their inhabitants the peculiar interests of those States cannot be secured under that Constitution. This pretended right, it will be perceived, strikes at once at the stability of all government, and every people in the world is interested in its rejection. Let us examine into the justness of the pretension, and also into the particular interests which are alleged to have demanded its assertion.

First, as to *the Right of Secession.* It is based upon the plea that the American Union is a simple Confederation or league of independent States which, for certain specified purposes, entered

[1] Putnam's *Rebellion Record,* New York, 1861, quoted also in Rawlins' "American Dis-Union," p. 18.

into an alliance. An examination into the history of the formation of the Constitution will prove, we think conclusively, the fallacy of this plea.

Between the years 1777 and 1788, the thirteen American colonies, which combined to resist the oppressive legislation of England, were united under certain articles of government, the title of which was "*Articles of Confederation and perpetual Union between the States* of New Hampshire, Massachusetts Bay, Rhode Island and Providence Plantations, Connecticut, New York, New Jersey, Pennsylvania, Delaware, Maryland, Virginia, North Carolina, South Carolina, and Georgia." The third of these Articles declared that "the said *States* hereby severally enter into *a firm league of friendship* with each other." Such a league may be formed at any time between independent States.

Each State was at liberty, with the consent of Congress, to establish its own custom-houses and revenue laws, to make alliances, to engage in war, to maintain military forces, to levy taxes and imposts, &c. &c.

No adequate provision was made for the enforcement, by the Congress, of such laws as the States in Congress assembled might enact. The revenues of the country were wholly under the control of the several States, and the only means on which the Congress could rely for the support of the Government were such voluntary grants as the States could be induced to make. In short, the Congress had no power whatever over the people, these being the subjects of the several States, neither had it any authority over the States themselves; it might request and advise, but it could not command them.

The insufficiency of such an union as this was painfully manifest during the war of independence even, when the strong bond of a common danger held the States together; the war ended, Congress commanded no reverence at home, and inspired no respect abroad. Powerless to compel the fulfilment, on the part of its own people, of the stipulations which, in their name, it had made with England at the conclusion of the war, that power refused in turn to execute the terms of the treaty. Washington himself wrote, "The Confederation appears to me little more than a shadow without substance, and Congress a nullity." And when the British Government was applied to by the American Commissioners, in 1785, to enter into a commercial treaty with the United States, the Duke of Dorset inquired of them whether they had been appointed by Congress, or their respective States, for it appeared to him "that each State was determined to manage matters its own way."

The inherent and essential vice of the original Confederacy was thus, manifestly and notoriously, the independent sovereignty of the States composing it, and the jealousy with which each maintained its independence; and also the absence of a proper relationship between the general Government and the people. The wise men of the country saw the necessity of a thorough change. Accordingly, after repeated and earnest appeals from the Congress and the several State Legislatures, a Convention of delegates from the States was held at Philadelphia, in 1787, "for the purpose of revising the Articles of Confederation and Perpetual Union between the United States of America, *in order to render them adequate to the preservation and support of the Union.*" The present Constitution is the result of the deliberations of that body, which submitted its work to Congress, accompanied by an explanatory letter, signed by Washington as President of the Convention. This letter declared, "It is obviously impracticable in the Federal Government of these States *to secure all rights of* independent sovereignty to each, and yet provide for the interest and safety of all. In all our deliberations we kept steadily in view that which appears to us the greatest interest of every true American—*the consolidation of our Union*—in which is involved our prosperity, safety, perhaps our national existence." These expressions prove conclusively the object which the illustrious framers of the Constitution had in preparing a substitute for the original Articles of Confederation; instead of a mere "firm league of friendship" between independent and jealous States, they wished to *constitute, to consolidate, a nation.* Hence they termed their work a "*Constitution.*"

This Constitution was transmitted by Congress to the Legislatures of the several States, by which, in turn, it was submitted to conventions of delegates, "chosen in each State by the people thereof." Thus, it passed out of the hands of the States into the hands of the people, by whom it was adopted and ratified in the following emphatic terms :—"We, *the People of the United States*, in order to form a more perfect Union (than the old firm league of friendship), establish justice, insure domestic tranquillity, provide for the common defence, promote the general welfare, and secure the blessings of liberty to ourselves and our posterity, do ordain and establish this Constitution for the United States of America."

It will escape no one that there are many capital differences between the new Constitution and the old Articles of Confederation. These differences strike at the very root, and are evidently intended to remedy the fundamental defects, of the latter,—State sovereignty, and the want of controlling authority of the general Government over the people. The Constitution considers itself not as emanating from the States, but as the creation of the people; from whom it derives, immediately, all its powers, and by whom it was constituted supreme not only over the States, but likewise over the people themselves, as to their persons and their property. Consequently the Constitution recognises the States only as convenient and authorized media of communication and action between itself and the people, so far as the relationship of the people to the National Government is concerned. This, we think, will be evident by comparing the new bond of union between the States with the old. The latter consisted simply of *Articles of Confederation;* the former is a *Constitution.* The old instrument only professed to establish "*a firm league of friendship*" between independent States; the new instrument ignores the States entirely, proclaiming itself to have been ordained and established by the people. The old bond was one of "Confederation and perpetual union;" the new declares its object to be "the formation of *a more perfect* Union," a union not of the States but of the people, while its framers themselves state that its aim was "*the consolidation of the Union.*"

But the differences between the old Articles of Confederation and the new Constitution do not stop here. The former declared, "*Each State retains its sovereignty, freedom, and independence,* and every power, jurisdiction, and right which is not by this Confederation expressly delegated to the United States in Congress assembled." But no such delegation was ever made, excepting as temporary loans by express agreement of at least nine of these independent sovereignties; and throughout the entire instrument the independence of the States was jealously declared and insisted on. The Constitution, on the other hand, sweeps away from the States and concentrates within itself for ever all the attributes of sovereignty, and delegates them at will; it expressly says, "The President, Congress, the Judiciary, *shall possess*" this, that, and the other right and power, and "*no State shall*" do so and so. Thus, the States, as independent sovereignties, disappear from the programme; as such they are not alluded to in the Constitution: the only passage which can be possibly construed into even an implication of their existence as such, occurs in an amendment to the original instrument, as follows:—"The powers not delegated to the United States by the Constitution, *nor prohibited by it to the States,* are reserved to the States respectively, *or to the people.*" (Art. X. of the Amendments.) Another Amendment (IX.) exhibits still more clearly the altered theory of government, as compared with that of the Articles of Confederation; it is as follows:—"The enumeration in the Constitution of certain rights shall not be construed to deny or discharge others *retained by the people.*" Thus, this new Evangel of political liberty proclaims unmistakably that, in government, all power comes exclusively from the people, and should be exercised solely for the benefit of the people.

The attributes and powers which the people thus reclaimed from the States, and conferred upon the Constitution of their adoption, are to levy and collect taxes, imposts, excises, &c.; to borrow, coin, and regulate the value of, money; to control foreign and domestic commerce; to enact naturalisation laws; to contract alliances and make treaties: to establish post-offices and post-roads; to declare war, and to make peace; to raise and support armies and fleets, &c. &c. Even the militia in the different States was directed to be "trained according to the discipline prescribed by Congress." Thus the people vested in the new Constitution the right to consider and treat themselves as its immediate subjects, placing themselves and their property under its direct control, abrogating in its favour the former exclusive sovereignty over themselves of their respective State Governments.

One of the first resolutions of the Convention which framed the Constitution was, "That a *National Government* ought to be established, consisting of a *supreme* Legislature, Executive, and Judiciary." And the more one studies the manner in which each of these departments was constituted, the more one is convinced of the supremacy of each, in its particular sphere, over the several States. Without attempting anything like a detailed examination, we desire to indicate one or two important points which appear to us to establish this view.

Under the Confederation there was no separate Executive branch of Government. The executive functions were performed by the Legislative body, the Congress, which consisted of from two to seven delegates from each State; but no important act of sovereignty could be performed by it, unless at least nine of the States in Congress assembled had assented to the same; and no other question could be decided, excepting that of daily adjournment, unless a majority of all the States (not a majority of the delegates) should have agreed thereto. During the recess of the Congress, the executive functions were devolved upon "a Committee of the States," appointed by the United States in Congress assembled, consisting of one of the delegates from each State. The Committee of the States, or any nine of them, were authorized to exercise such of the powers of Congress "as the United States in Congress assembled, by the consent of nine States, should, from time to time, think it expedient to vest them with; provided that no power be delegated to the said Committee for the exercise of which, by the Articles of Confederation, the voice of nine States in the Congress of the United States assembled is requisite." The sovereignty of the States was thus most jealously guarded.

On the other hand, under the Constitution a *Presidency* was established, as the Executive department of the Government. The President was directed to be chosen by a majority of the Electors appointed directly *by the people* for this very purpose; and in the event of a majority of these electors not being able to agree upon any one person, the President was then to be chosen (not by the Senate, which represents, to a certain extent, the States, but) by the House of Representatives of the people. Thus the executive head of the nation was elected directly by the people—the States, as States, having nothing to do with his election.

It is pretended that the old supremacy of the States has been virtually recognised and perpetuated under the Constitution, in the mode of organization of the Senate. The Senate, which did not exist under the Articles of Confederation, consists, under the Constitution, of two persons chosen (not by the people, but) by the Legislature of each State; and the consent of the Senate is made necessary to the validity of most of the acts of the President, and of the measures passed by the House of Representatives, before these can become laws. But this plea amounts to nothing, because the members of the State Legislatures who elect the United States senators are themselves chosen directly by the people of the States. Moreover, the presiding officer of the Senate, who, in the event of a tie-vote among the senators, has a controlling vote over their deliberations, is the Vice-President of the United States, elected by the people themselves, as is the President.

The supremacy of the Constitution over the States is still farther proclaimed as follows:—"This Constitution and the laws of the United States which shall be made in pursuance thereof, and all treaties made, or which shall be made, under the authority of the United States, *shall be the supreme law of the land;* and the judges in every State shall be bound thereby, anything in the Constitution or laws of any State to the contrary notwithstanding. The senators and representatives before mentioned (of the United States), and the members of the several State Legislatures, and all the executive and judicial officers, both of the United States and the several States, shall be bound by oath or affirmation to support this Constitution." (Art. VI.)

Amongst the various powers vested in the Constitution and delegated by it to Congress is that of "calling forth the militia to execute the laws of the Union, suppress insurrections, and repel invasions." (Art. I. Sect. 8.) Now, what is *Secession* but insurrection against the laws of the Union? Is it not absurd, then, to pretend that a State possesses, under or from the Constitution, the right of secession, when that very Constitution imposes upon Congress the duty of "calling forth the militia to execute the laws of the Union and suppress insurrection"?

Moreover, it was the universal conviction, both of the friends and the enemies of this new Constitution, that it did absorb all the sovereign attributes which heretofore had been claimed and exercised by the several States of the Confederation. And such continued to be the general opinion until within the last thirty years, at the South as well as at the North. In fact, Mr. Benton,[1] a slave-holding senator, has left on record that, until that period, "the leading language south of the Potomac was, that no State had a right to withdraw from the Union; that it required the same power to dissolve as to form the Union; and that any attempt to dissolve it, or to obstruct the action of constitutional laws, was treason."

The Supreme Court, soon after its organization as the legal interpreter and expounder of the Constitution, held the following language in an important case which was submitted to its decision:[2] "It has been said that the States were sovereign, were completely independent, and were connected with each other by a league. This is true. But when those allied sovereignties converted their league into a Government, when they converted their Congress of Ambassadors into a Legislature empowered to enact laws, the whole character in which the States appear underwent a change." Such has been the unvarying decision of the Supreme Court, even of those branches of it which belong to Southern districts.

The public men of the South formerly entertained no doubt on this question. In the Convention of the people of Virginia, Jefferson, who was one of the framers of the Constitution, opposed its adoption on the ground that it did assume supremacy over the States. Patrick Henry,[3] before the same Convention, opposed its adoption for the same reason, saying, "*If the States be not the agents of this compact, it must be one great consolidated National Government of the people of all the States.*" And, again, "Have the framers of this Constitution made a proposal of compact between *the States?* If they had this would be a confederation; it is, otherwise, most clearly *a Consolidated Government.* The whole question turns on that poor little expression, '*We, the people,*' instead of *the States* of America." Mr. Madison,[4] one of the most prominent of the framers of the instrument, said of it, before the same Convention, "Should all the States adopt it, it will then be a Government established by the Thirteen States of America, *not*

[1] See Ludlow's "History of the United States," p. 103.
[2] "Causes of the American Civil War," by Mr. Motley, p. 10.
[3] Wirt's "Life of Patrick Henry," quoted by Rawlins, op. cit. pp. 63, 64.
[4] Rawlins, p. 65.

through the intervention of the Legislatures, but by the people at large." Mason,[1] in the same Convention, opposed it as follows:—"Whether the Constitution be good or bad, the present clause (the preamble) clearly discovers that it is to be *a National Government and no longer a Confederation of States.*" Mr. Pinckney,[2] on the other hand, in the Convention of the people of South Carolina, advocated its adoption for this very reason:—"This admirable manifesto sufficiently refutes the doctrine of the individual sovereignty and independence of the States."

After full discussion in conventions of the people of the several States, the Constitution was adopted by all. Judge Story declares that "there was no reservation of any right on the part of any State to dissolve its connexion, or to abrogate its assent, or to suspend, as to itself, the operation of the Constitution." It was felt and acknowledged that it was adapted to and required by the exigences of the times. All over the land the people approved of it; they felt that, to acquiesce any longer in the doctrine of the sovereignty of the several States, was to commit political suicide.

But, it is frequently said, the American people threw off the supremacy of Great Britain because it was no longer agreeable to them; should their descendants be compelled to submit to the Federal Constitution after it had ceased to subserve their interests? We reply, the Colonists rebelled against the oppressive acts of a Government and a Legislature in which they were not represented. The South has never been oppressed; it has governed the country, in virtue, partly, of its superabundant representation in the National Legislature—the slaves who, at the South, are regarded as mere *chattels*, being counted as *men* in elections for Congressional Representatives, three-fifths of the slaves being added to the number of the white population of the slave States. Moreover, the Constitution itself provides proper methods for remedying its own defects, and all grievances which may have arisen from abuse or mal-administration of its provisions. (Art. V.) The Constitution has also established a National Judiciary having jurisdiction over all "controversies to which the United States shall be a party; controversies

[1] Elliott's Debates, quoted by Mr. Sumner, on *Our Domestic Relations*, p. 513.

[2] Quoted in Ludlow's "History of the United States," p. 14.

between two or more States; between a State and citizens of another State," &c. &c. (Art. III.) The seceding States did not resort to any of the constitutional methods thus provided for the redress of their asserted grievances.

The advocates of the modern doctrine of State sovereignty lay much stress upon the declaration made by the delegates of the people of Virginia, assembled in Convocation to decide upon the adoption or rejection of the proposed Constitution, in 1788, in the following words:—"The powers under the Constitution *being derived from the people of the United States, may be resumed by them* whenever the same shall be perverted to their injury or oppression." We admit this declaration; and the Constitution, as we have just stated, points out the mode by which "the people of the United States" should make their desires known. But this is a very different doctrine from that of State sovereignty; indeed, it is completely subversive of the latter. Neither did the seceding States act according to this principle thus formally announced by one of themselves. Not only was the vast majority of "the people of the United States" not consulted on the subject, but they were known to be, and are still, violently opposed to secession. Secession was accomplished by a very small minority of the people of a minority of the States. The question was not submitted at all to *the people* of some of the seceding States; in all of them it was warmly opposed, and was carried affirmatively only by means of gross violence and intimidation.[1] It is believed, even at the South, that a very large majority of the people were opposed to secession. At the Presidential election of 1860, Mr. Breckenridge, the Candidate of the Southern Extremists, received in all the Slave States 436,592 votes; the other candidates, who were all avowed Unionists, holding different views with regard to the extension of slavery into the territories, received 419,932 votes. If it could have been foreseen that a civil war would have followed upon that election, there is every reason to believe that an overwhelming majority of the people of the Slave States would have voted in support of the Union candidates. In Virginia the vote was 92,900 in their favour, against 74,323;

[1] Speeches of Southern refugees at New York, in October, 1862, particularly those of Texans; *Revue des deux Mondes*, December, 1860; *Annuaire des deux Mondes*, 1860; &c. &c.

in Tennessee 80,624, against 64,709; in Louisiana 27,829, against 22,681; even in Georgia 54,476, against 51,889. Throughout the South many of the most respectable journals did not hesitate to characterize the secession movement as the work of ambitious politicians whose views found no sympathy with the majority of the people.[1] Mr. Stephens, the actual Vice-President of the Confederacy, held substantially the same language in his speech before the Convention of Georgia, from which we have already quoted. Even in the South Carolina Convention, Mr. Boyce declared:—"If secession shall take place, of which I have no idea—for I cannot conceive of such stupendous madness—I shall consider the institution of slavery as doomed, and that the great God, in our blindness, has made us the instruments of its destruction." The perils of the step were fully exposed by some of the most prominent public men of the South, and by some of the leading journals. Thus *The Raleigh Standard*, of North Carolina, depicted "the fearful evils which must result from secession—repudiation, bankruptcy, beggary, the predominance of the sword over law, and, the end, abolition." But secession was determined upon by the leaders of the movement.

We have dwelt at considerable length on this question of the right of secession, partly on account of its intrinsic interest, and partly because so much importance has been ascribed to it by the advocates of the South in England. Evidently there is no such right to be deduced either from the Constitution of the United States or from the circumstances which led to its formation, or from the intentions of its founders.[2]

[1] *Annuaire des deux Mondes*, 1860, pp. 606, 608; Ellison, "Slavery and Secession," p. 67; Story, "The American Question," &c. &c.

[2] The preamble of the Confederate Constitution is as follows: "We, the People of the *Confederate* States, *each State acting in its sovereign and independent character*, in order to form a *Permanent Federal Government*," &c. We have italicised the words which differ from those used in the preamble of the United States Constitution. Now, the Confederate Constitution is almost a verbatim copy of the Constitution of the United States, excepting in certain points. It is evident that, in those points, the wording has been made to differ for the express purpose of creating a corresponding change of meaning and principle. Thus the preamble of the Confederate Constitution shows of itself unmistakably that the Government constituted by that instrument was intended by its framers to differ *essentially* from that established under the Constitution of the United States. The former was intended to be a *Federal* Government over *Confederate States*, "each State acting in its sovereign and independent character." This is

But if the original States of the Union, those which ratified the Constitution at the time of its adoption, can claim no such right, much less can those other States which have entered the Union since that period. The settlers of the present States of Arkansas, Tennessee, Mississippi, and Alabama, were allowed by the Federal Government to occupy lands within those States when these were territories governed by Congress under the Constitution. When the population of these territories had become sufficiently numerous, they were severally admitted as States, each one having previously submitted its Constitution to Congress for sanction. These States, therefore, never possessed any rights which they did not acquire under the authorization and sanction of the Federal Government; surely no one can pretend that one of those rights could have been to violate the Constitution by subverting that Government.

Again, Florida and Louisiana were purchased—the one from Spain, the other from France—out of the common treasury of the United States. The chief stipulation in the treaty of purchase, besides that referring to the payment of the purchase-money, was that the inhabitants of those territories should not be deprived of the rights which they possessed under their old Governments. Very certainly one of those rights was not that of throwing off their allegiance whenever they might see fit: France and Spain conferred no such right upon their subjects.

Finally, who is authorized, under the Constitution, to sanction or permit the rupture of the Union? The President and all the other officers of the Government, the members of Congress, the judges of the courts, the officers of the army and navy, the governor, legislators and judges of each State, are each and all bound, by solemn oath or affirmation, to uphold the Constitution of the United States as "the supreme law of the

nothing more than "a firm league of friendship and perpetual union," as was that formed under the old Articles of Confederation. We may expect, therefore, to find similar results to follow this new attempt at establishing such a Government, as those which were witnessed under its prototype. The differences which we have pointed out may be taken as strong presumptive proof that the framers of the Confederate Constitution were convinced that the Constitution of the United States was drawn up with a different intention from that which governed and actuated themselves in their work, and that it contains no such principle as the sovereignty and independence of the several States, which constitutes the basis of their own.

land," ordained and established for the declared purpose of forming a Union "more perfect" than that secured by the *Articles of Confederation* which itself declared "the Union shall be perpetual."[1]

Our English friends have freely counselled us that it was better to let the South go rather than encounter the evils of civil war. They have never acted, and probably it will be long ere they will act, upon this principle themselves. Sir Robert Peel said, in 1843, at the time of the Irish agitation for the repeal of the Union: "Deprecating as I do all war, and especially civil war, yet there is no alternative which I do not think preferable to the dismemberment of the British empire." But what an insignificant loss would the loss of Ireland have been to Great Britain, compared with that of the Southern States to the rest of the Union. The former event would have left no long line of frontier exposed; it would have involved no increase of military forces, nor of custom-house officials; it would have occasioned the giving up of no immense line of internal navigation to the command of an enemy; nor would it have annihilated the cohesive affinities of the remaining elements of the empire. The loss of Ireland, from a repeal of the Union, would, in all probability, have been a temporary loss only; the successful revolt of the Southern States would be an immense and a permanent evil to the United States, not so much from the mere material diminution of territory and population, as for other reasons just hinted at. And besides, it would be the prelude to the establishment of a military "Slave Republic," before whose rapacity and despotism all that we read of Roman or Moslem dominion pales.

Secondly, as to the *grievances* which the English admirers of the South allege in justification of the rebellion. We have already quoted the testimony of the Southern Vice-President in proof that there was no sufficient grievance; nevertheless, we desire to refute the two most important charges made against

[1] On the question of the Right of Secession, consult "The Madison Papers;" Elliott's "Debates;" *The Federalist*; Story's "Commentaries, &c.;" also the following recent pamphlets:—"Causes of the American Civil War," by Hon. J. L. Motley, London, 1861; "The American Question," by W. W. Story, London, 1862; An Article on "*Our Domestic Relations*," by Mr. Sumner, in the *Atlantic Monthly Magazine*, Oct. 1863; "The League of States," by B. J. Lossing, New York, 1863; Bacon's "Guide to American Politics," London, 1863; Rawlins on "American Dis-Union," London, 1862, a most able and critical *resumé* of the question.

the North, the non-execution of the Fugitive-Slave laws, and the imposition of oppressive and injurious Tariffs.

The Fugitive-Slave Laws. The original clause in the Constitution concerning the return of fugitive slaves is as follows: "No person held to service or labour in one State, under the laws thereof, escaping into another, shall, in consequence of any law or regulation therein, be discharged from such service or labour, but shall be delivered on claim of the party to whom such service or labour is due." (Art. IV. Sect. 2.) The enacting of this clause was not accompanied by any grant of power to enforce it; it stands on the same footing as the clause immediately preceding it, on the rendition of fugitives from justice, namely, as a compact between the States, to be fulfilled on the requisition of the Executive of the State from which the criminal or the fugitive may have escaped.

In 1793, five years after the Constitution was adopted, an Act was passed providing, for the first time, for the execution of both these clauses. So little attention did the subject excite, however, that, it is said, twenty-six years elapsed before a single slave was surrendered under the Act.[1] Indeed, the whole history of the introduction of the original clause into the Constitution, shows that, as Mr. Sumner says, the slave-owners attached but very little importance to the matter.

In 1801, a motion was made in Congress to substitute a new Act for that of 1793, but the idea was abandoned, as was also another attempt made in 1817-18.

In 1850, at the time of the admission of California as a free State, the present fugitive-slave law was enacted, as an important element of a series of compromise measures. Its author was Mr. Mason, of Virginia, late Confederate Commissioner to London.

We admit that it has always been difficult to enforce these laws; in many instances attempts to execute them have failed, partly by the interference of the people, partly by the refusal of the State officials to lend any assistance whatever to the officers of the general Government, and partly in consequence of the interposition by the States of direct obstacles. We by no means wish to uphold either individuals or societies in

[1] Mr. Sumner's Speech on his motion to repeal the Fugitive-Slave Act of 1850, in the Senate, 1852.

disobedience to any law of the land. We desire to point out, however, that there are very many facts connected with the laws in question, which explain and palliate the opposition made to them.

The law of 1793 was, in the judgment of the Supreme Court, radically defective, inasmuch as it devolved its enforcement upon State authorities. It was a Federal law, and, consequently, ought to depend for its execution upon Federal judges and officers.[1]

The law of 1850 is open to still more grave objections. By its language it makes no discrimination as to colour, race or class, beyond the sweeping designation of "persons held to service or labour;" it commits the decision of the claim, on the part of the owner of the slave, to the judgment of a mere petty magistrate appointed by the Court, holding office only during the pleasure of the Court, receiving no fixed salary, and exposed to the temptation of giving a dishonest judgment by the promise of a double fee, if he should condemn the fugitive to be returned to slavery. But, more monstrous still, it refuses to the defendant the privilege of *habeas corpus* and of trial by jury. On these two last grounds the law has been pronounced unconstitutional.

As to the writ of *habeas corpus;* it is ordered by the Constitution that "the privilege of the writ of *habeas corpus* shall not be suspended, unless when in cases of rebellion or invasion the public safety may require it" (Art. I. Sect. 9). This provision must, of course, apply to all persons, and by the Constitution even slaves are persons.

The Constitution of the United States expressly terms slaves *persons* (Art. I. Sect. 2); even the fugitive-slave clause of the Constitution speaks of the slave as a *person.*[2] The Constitution farther declares that "*no person* shall be deprived of life, *liberty,* or property, *without due process of law*" (Art. V.); now, as all negroes, or persons of colour, found in the free States are presumably free, they cannot, according to this provision, be deprived of their liberty without due process of law. Again, the Constitution provides that, "in suits at common law, where the value in controversy shall exceed twenty dollars, *the right of trial by jury shall be preserved*" (Amendments, Art. VII.); upon

[1] Mr. Sumner's Speech.

[2] See the clause already quoted.

this clause also the law might be resisted, for it may safely be predicated that the value of any runaway slave, whom his owner would take the trouble to reclaim, would "exceed twenty dollars."

The Supreme Court of the United States[1] has given the following recorded decisions, which seem to be incompatible with the fugitive-slave law of 1850: 1st. That "a suit is the prosecution of some *claim*, demand, or request." The claim of a master for an alleged fugitive slave is, then, *a suit;* 2d. That *suits at common law* comprise, "not merely suits which the common law recognises among its old and settled proceedings, but suits in which *legal rights* are to be ascertained and determined." Certainly, then, the ascertaining and determining the right of a person to his liberty must be done by a suit at common law; 3d. In a case in which the appellants were petitioners for freedom, the Supreme Court said: "The matter in dispute is the freedom of the petitioners. This is not susceptible of pecuniary valuation. No doubt is entertained of the jurisdiction of the Court." We may, therefore, safely contend that the fugitive-slave law of 1850 is an unconstitutional law, inasmuch as it ignores, to the prejudice of alleged fugitive slaves, who are persons in the eye of the Constitution, the all-important rights to the privileges of *habeas corpus* and trial by jury, to which that instrument entitles them.

But not only did this law appear to the people of the free States a flagrant violation of the Constitution, against liberty and in favour of slavery; it outraged them in other ways. It was retrospective in its operation, without any limit as to time; slaves whose owner had died since their escape, could be claimed by a new master, whose property they had become by inheritance, or by purchase. More than this. So hostile had the modern legislation of the slave States become to emancipation, that slaves who had virtually been freed by their masters, and who had every right to consider themselves free, were liable, in consequence of some flaw in their manumission, to be pursued and claimed, either by State authorities, or by some new owner, or pretended owner. So great was the terror which the passage of the law excited amongst the coloured immigrants in the free States, that no one considered himself safe, no matter how long

[1] Mr. Sumner's Speech.

he might have resided therein. "Mr. Palfrey[1] says that 130 communicants of a single church in Buffalo, New York, escaped to Canada; that the coloured Baptist church in Rochester, in the same State, lost all but two of its 114 communicants; that the coloured Baptist church in Detroit, Michigan, lost eighty-four communicants."

Again, as Mr. Sumner finely observes, "The law lacked that essential support in the Public Conscience of the States in which it was to be enforced, which is the life of all law, and without which all law must become a dead letter." Every human being in those States felt that a poor wretch, "God's image, though carved in ebony," who, to escape a slave's chain, or a slave's punishment, or the recollection of a slave's punishment, had surmounted all the difficulties in the way of his deliverance—the swamp, the forest, the armed patrol, the chance passer-by, the hunger and thirst, the hunter and the hounds,—had richly earned the right to be free for ever.[2]

The religious sentiment also of the free States was outraged by this law. Thanks to Southern agitation, every one there had learned that the Bible declares to him, "Thou shalt not deliver unto his master the servant which is escaped from his master unto thee; he shall dwell with thee, even among you, in that place which he shall choose in one of thy gates, where it liketh him best." The modern apologists for Slavery, one of the latest of whom is the London *Times*, pretend, indeed, that St. Paul gives a later and a more reliable revelation of the mind of the Almighty, and directs that fugitive slaves shall be restored to their masters. But we are persuaded that any one, not a slave-holder, who will carefully read the celebrated epistle of St. Paul to Philemon, can draw from it only this conviction, viz.: that *no Christian* has a right to hold a fellow-Christian as a slave, but that he is commanded to substitute for the Pagan and Jewish chain of slavery the Christian bond of brotherhood; to look upon a slave as *no more " a servant, but above a servant, a brother beloved."*

But notwithstanding all these legitimate objections to the fugitive-slave law, on the part of the people of the free States

[1] Ludlow's "History of the United States," p. 242.

[2] See remarks of Mr. Olmsted on the hardships and dangers encountered by runaway negroes, in his "Travels through the Seaboard Slave States," pp. 159-163, &c.

it was the law, and they submitted to it. In the vast majority of instances in which a fugitive was claimed, and the claim properly authenticated and established, he was permitted to be taken away by his owner. After all, the grievance was pitifully small. The Superintendent of the Census Bureau states that in 1860, only 803 Slaves made their escape out of the almost 4,000,000 of servile population—a little more than one-fiftieth of one per cent. Many of these took refuge in the everglades and swamps of Florida, North Carolina and other Slave states; many betook themselves to Mexico; a very small proportion found shelter in the free States and in Canada. Moreover, if the escape and the non-recovery of fugitive slaves has been a grievance under the Union, of which the law was made to favour the owner, what would be the case if the South should become independent and surrounded by free States all favourable to the runaway?

It is evident, then, that the grievance complained of was trifling, as against the North, and that the remedy which the South has applied to it is an infinite aggravation, so far as the mere loss of slave property is concerned. The non-compliance with the fugitive-slave law was urged, not as a grievance against the North, but as a convenient pretext for exciting the jealousy and animosity of the slave-owners and their adherents. That this is the fact, is evident from the manner in which Mr. Stephens alludes to the matter, in the quotation we have already given from his speech, Moreover, in the Convention of South Carolina which determined upon secession, in 1860, Mr. Rhett declares, "Secession is nothing produced by Mr. Lincoln's election *or the non-execution of the fugitive-slave law.* It is a matter which has been gathering head for thirty years."[1] Other speakers corroborated this statement.

It often happens that those who are most indignant at any and every infraction of the law against themselves, are the least observant of their own duties, and least considerate of the rights of others. So it has been in the conduct of the slave-owners. All over the slave States, Northern travellers and residents, guiltless of any intention or desire to interfere in any way with "the peculiar institution," free even from any taint of abolitionism, have in many instances been subjected to annoyance, ill-treatment, personal violence, and forcible ejection from the

[1] Speech of Mr. Sumner, on the Rebellion, &c., Nov. 27, 1861.

State in which they happened to be ; others have been put to death. The mails have been violated in search of suspected abolition documents, newspapers or private letters. Southern journals have repeatedly advocated the promise of a pecuniary reward for the heads of well-known Northern men opposed to slavery ; the head of Mr. Seward, the present Secretary of State, was appraised at fifty thousand dollars. Public meetings at the South have advocated similar proceedings ; a committee of vigilance of Louisiana, in 1835, offered, in the *Louisiana Journal*, fifty thousand dollars to any one who would deliver into their hands Arthur Tappan, a merchant of New York ; in the same year a public meeting in Alabama offered a similar reward for the delivery to them of Arthur Tappan, and a Methodist clergyman, of New York. In 1831, the Legislature of Georgia passed a law, and the Governor of the State approved of it, appropriating five thousand dollars "to be paid to any person who shall arrest, bring to trial, and prosecute to conviction under the laws of this State, the editor or publisher of a certain paper called the *Liberator*, published at the town of Boston and State of Massachusetts." The editor in question had never set his foot in Georgia, and in his journal he had sedulously and on principle abstained from any appeal to the slaves themselves. The halls of the National Congress were frequently the theatre of similar denunciations. Senator Hammond, of South Carolina, said, "I warn the abolitionists, ignorant infatuated barbarians as they are, that if chance shall throw any of them into our hands, they may expect a felon's death."[1]

South Carolina was the only State whose ordinance justifying secession makes special mention of the non-execution of the fugitive-slave law as a grievance against the North.[2] The most important charge made in this manifesto, that "in none of the free States has the State Government complied with the stipulations made in the Constitution" concerning the restoration of fugitive slaves, is notoriously untrue. But South Carolina, of all the slave States, has the least reason to complain, even of this, because she has suffered little, if any, loss by the escape of slaves. South Carolina, of all the States of the Union, has the

[1] Speech of Mr. Sumner, on the Barbarism of Slavery, United States' Senate, 1860.

[2] Bacon's "Guide to American Politics," p. 54.

smallest right, from her own example, to find fault with any other of being unfaithful to any constitutional obligation. Lukewarm in fighting the War of Independence from 1775 to 1783;[1] reluctant in adopting the Constitution in 1788; unscrupulous violator of the Constitution since 1823,[2] by the enactment and enforcement of a law under which all free persons of colour, though citizens of the North, arriving at the port of Charleston have been imprisoned until the departure of the ship to which they belonged, and, in default of payment of the expenses of their detention, have been liable to "be seized and taken as absolute slaves;" again violating the Constitution by passing another law which deprives these citizens of the North of the privilege of the writ of *haheas corpus;* violating again the spirit, not only of the Constitution of the United States, but of all merciful and humane legislation, by another statute, forbidding, under severe penalties, any person in the State from accepting a commission to befriend these oppressed seamen, and prohibiting, under the penalty even of imprisonment for life, "any person, on his own behalf, or by virtue of any authority from any State, to enter

[1] The vote of South Carolina was at first given *against* the Declaration of Independence, and her assent was finally obtained only for the sake of securing a seeming unanimity in favour of that Act (Speech of Senator Sumner, New York, Nov. 27, 1861). During the war of the Revolution, South Carolina, with a population of 249,073 (in 1790), furnished only 5,508 Continental troops and militia for the general defence; while Massachusetts, with a population of 378,717 (in 1790), furnished 83,092 of such soldiers. The Southern States, with an aggregate population of 1,852,504 (in 1790), of which, perhaps, 650,000 were slaves (the slave population of all the States, in 1790, was 697,897), furnished 71,130 soldiers for the Revolutionary War; the Northern States, with an aggregate population of 1,786,489, provided 218,553 soldiers. ("Report of the Governor of Massachusetts," Feb. 3, 1863, compared with the "National Almanac," of 1863, p. 307.

[2] Mr. Sumner's "Speech on the Barbarism of Slavery," pp. 51–53. The Constitution declares that "The citizens of each State shall be entitled to all the privileges and immunities of citizens in the several States." (Art. IV. Sect. II.) Now, at the time of the adoption of the Constitution, all free, native-born inhabitants of New Hampshire, Massachusetts, New York, New Jersey, and even of North Carolina, even though descended from African slaves, were not only citizens of those States, but voted on equal terms with other citizens. (See the Opinion of Mr. Justice Curtis, in the Dred Scott case, quoted by Mr. Livermore in his "Historical Research," Boston, 1863.) Consequently, so far as the free negroes of those States were concerned, the law of South Carolina violated the Constitution, as was declared at the time by the Attorney-General of the United States, a Virginian, and by Mr. Justice Johnson, of the Supreme Court, a South Carolinian. (Mr. Sumner's Speech, p. 51.)

the State of South Carolina for a similar purpose;[1] in open arms against the Constitution in 1832, on the Tariff question: South Carolina has been always, and at all times the *âme damné* of all hostility to the Constitution of the United States, the fomenter of discord, sectional hatred, and disunion. The slave States, least of all South Carolina, had no right, therefore, to expect that the North would show them any favour against fugitives from slavery. The Northern people exercised not only their legal right, but performed their duty to humanity, in insisting in every instance that the claimant of the fugitive should establish his claim in the most unimpeachable manner, before they consented to the surrender of the victim.

The Tariff. In the United States, no one pretended that the South was injured or aggrieved by the Tariff system. No allusion whatever is made to this in any of the Southern manifestoes justifying their secession. It was invented exclusively for foreign, especially for English, markets.

The mere fact, which is universally admitted, and which is convincingly established by Mr. Stephens, in the speech from which we have quoted, that the South has had the government of the United States in its own hands, would be sufficient proof that, if the slave States have been the victims of the Tariff policy, they have been willing victims. But this fact can be otherwise demonstrated.

In 1789, in the first session of Congress, after the adoption of the Constitution, one of the first measures proposed was a Bill levying duties on foreign goods imported, "for the support of Government, for the discharge of the public debt, *and the encouragement and protection of manufactures.*" All the Southern Congressmen voted in favour of this Bill. The leader of the House was Mr. Madison, of Virginia. In 1790, the duties were increased by the votes of 88 per cent. of the Southern and of 60 per cent. of the Northern Representatives. In 1794, an unanimous vote imposed an additional impost. In 1797, imposts were again augmented by 79 per cent. of Northern, and 71 per cent. of Southern votes. In 1804, an unanimous Southern vote, with 61 per cent. of Northern votes, imposed additional duties. In 1812, a further increase of imposts was directed by 73 per cent. of Southern, and 51 per cent. of Northern Representatives, 75 per

[1] Mr. Sumner's "Speech on the Barbarism of Slavery."

cent. of Southern, and 62 per cent of Northern Senators. Previous to this date, the vote in the Senate had been unanimous in favour of augmentations of duties. In 1816 a new increase was voted by the Senate unanimously; in the House, by 80 per cent. of the Northern, and 39 per cent. of the Southern delegation, led by Mr. Calhoun himself. This was pre-eminently a *protective Tariff.*

In 1824, under the leading of Mr. Clay, of slave-holding Kentucky, a permanent system, as it was intended, of protection was inaugurated. The Senate passed the Bill without a division; in the House of Representatives it was carried by only *three* votes, while *nineteen* votes were given in favour of it by Southern representatives. Again, in 1828, the average rate of duties was increased several per cent. by the votes of 26 per cent. of Southern, and 82 per cent. of Northern, Senators, and 21 per cent. of Southern, and 75 per cent. of Northern, Representatives. In the House of Representatives it was carried by a majority of *eleven* votes, while *seventeen* Southern Representatives supported the measure. Even in 1835, a *reduction* in the rate of imposts was *opposed* by 38 per cent. of Southern, and only 32 per cent. of Northern, Representatives.[1]

Northern capital had at first been most largely invested in commerce; but as the tendency of Congressional legislation seemed to be getting more and more favourable to the protection of domestic manufactures, Northern capitalists devoted more and more of their means to that branch of industry. On the contrary, gradually at the South public opinion became opposed to protection. Mr. Benton,[2] long a Senator from the slave State of Missouri, gives the following explanation of this change. He says that, in the colonial days, the South had been richer than the North; but, as time wore on, "Northern towns became great cities, Southern States remained stationary, or actually decayed, and Charlston, the principal port of the South, was less flourishing before than after the Revolution, and this in spite of a Southern export, since that event, to the value of eight hundred millions of dollars." The South, though possessing infinite resources and appliances for the establishment of manufacturing industry, including the monopoly of cotton, became convinced

[1] See a full report of the votes on the American Tariff Bills, in the London *Daily News*, Sept. 8, 1863.

[2] Ludlow's "History of the United States," pp. 12-34.

that her people could never become anything more than producers of *raw material* for other nations. Then, as since, her retrogression was ascribed, by herself, to the imposts which she herself had originated and maintained. But, as Mr. Benton shows, a protective tariff was really established only in 1816, while the decay of the South had been steadily accelerating since the Revolutionary War, under the ban and blight of an ever-increasing slave population.

The highest rate of protection ever imposed was by the Bill of 1842, which was supported by 26 per cent. of Northern, and 18 per cent. of Southern, Representatives; amongst the latter was Mr. Stephens, the actual Vice-President of the Southern Confederacy, who *opposed the repeal* of this law in 1846. In short, the South could at any time have prevented the enactment of any law for high imposts, had her Congressmen united with the Northern opponents of such a measure. But this has never been the case. Hence Mr. Calhoun,[1] always meditating schemes for securing Southern independence, in furtherance of slavery, exclaimed in 1833, that it was impossible to unite the Southern States on the Tariff question, and that thenceforth the basis of a common Southern opposition to the North must be sought for in slavery.

Mr. Stephens, in his speech before the Georgia Convention, placed this pretended grievance of the South in its true light, as follows:[2]—"When I entered public life in 1832, South Carolina threatened to leave the Union on the Tariff question; but the difficulty was smoothed down, and we have not had, since 1833, any cause of complaint. The present tariff (of 1857) was voted for by South Carolina as well as Massachusetts. It is, therefore, untrue to say that the South is obliged to pay arbitrary duties imposed by the North, since the Representatives of Massachusetts were unanimous in modifying those duties as the South desired."

[1] Ludlow's "History of the United States," p. 148.

It is interesting to note that the South was willing enough that the chief part (86 per cent.) of the Public Debt resulting from the War of the Revolution and of 1812, should be paid by the North in the shape of Customs and Revenue. It was not until 1833, when this Debt had been paid, and all fear of a resort to direct taxation had passed away, that Mr. Calhoun, who had voted in favour of the Tariff Bill of 1816, took ground against the hitherto received policy of the country, which the South had itself established.

[2] See "Les États-Unis en 1863," par M. Bigelow, Paris, 1863.

Thus a tariff for protection to domestic manufactures was originally a Southern measure, and the South has always advocated a tariff for revenue. Why? Simply because *it is for the interest of the slave States that the Government should be supported by a system of indirect rather than of direct taxation.* According to the Constitution, direct taxes are to be levied, not only upon the free population of the States, but also upon "three-fifths of all other persons," *i.e.* slaves (Art. I. Sect. 2). Consequently this mode of collecting a revenue would fall most heavily upon the slave States. Not only would the poor whites, who form, as we shall hereafter show, much the largest class of the white population of those States, be taxed beyond their means (of which they have none), but the small body of slave-owners would be compelled to pay for their millions of slaves. They felt, at the time of the formation of the Constitution, that this would be a burden too grievous to be borne. And even now, though the finances of the South are in need of every cent which can be obtained, the legislators, who are at the same time the proprietors of the land and of the slaves, have hitherto refused to allow that this property shall be taxed. On the other hand, under the operation of the tariff system of the Union, the population of the slave States have been obliged to pay for the support of the Government only in proportion to the amount of foreign merchandise which they have voluntarily purchased. Mr. Stephens, in his speech, has stated that amount at *less than one-third* of that paid by the Northern people. This astonishing fact, after all the assertions concerning this pretended grievance, will be readily understood, when we shall have contrasted the character and condition of the two populations, as we shall do on subsequent pages.

Thus, then, the tariff, so far from being a discriminating tax, levied by the North at the expense of the South, has been just the reverse. In all the legislation on this subject, the South has had the advantage of sending to the general Congress a representation based, according to the Constitution (Art. I. Sec. 2), not only upon its white population, but also upon three-fifths of its slaves, thereby increasing its congressional vote. And, inasmuch as all taxes levied upon commodities for consumption must necessarily fall upon the consumers of the same, these taxes have been paid chiefly by the thriving and industrious free population of the North, and not by the few slave-owners, and the millions of poor whites and slaves of the South, who consume a very small amount of taxable commodities. If the tariff has been oppressive, the oppression has been borne—and willingly borne—by the North. The tariff laws have, indeed, materially lessened the expenses of the Southern proprietors and the whole Southern white population in two ways:—*First,* they have reduced the quota of Southern contributions far below what they would have been under a system of direct taxation; and they have levied these contributions upon that class only of the population which was able to pay them (in exchange for foreign luxuries consumed). *Secondly,* by the aid and stimulus given to domestic industry, they have enabled the American manufacturer to supply the mass of the population, including the slaves, with all the articles which they need, at a lower rate than these could have been made abroad and delivered at the South. In fact, the coarse cottons and woollens, the shoes, the agricultural implements and machinery, the domestic utensils and tools for mechanics, such as are most needed in the slave States, are manufactured in America, and sold in English colonial markets cheaper than they can be supplied from England. Hence, even in the event of Southern independence, self-interest will compel the South to supply most of its wants from the Northern States.

As to "the infamous Morrill Tariff," it was itself an effect of secession; it could never have been adopted, had Southern Congressmen remained in Washington.

We are thus brought to consider the only serious cause of discord and disunion which has existed between the North and the South, viz. "*the peculiar institution*" of the latter, and the principles and policy which it has engendered. This has always been a source of disagreement between the people of the two sections. It was this which made some of the Southern Colonies lukewarm, if not hostile, towards the war for Independence.[1] It was this which made the Carolinas and Georgia

[1] John Adams said in a letter to General Gates, in 1776, "All our misfortunes arise from a single source: *the resistance of the Southern Colonies to Republican Government.*" (Adams' Works, vol. i. p. 207.) During the Revolutionary War, Baron de Kalb expressed surprise to General Marion, a South Carolina patriot, that "so many South Carolinians were running to take British protection." General Marion replied as follows: "The people of Carolina form two classes—the rich and the poor. The rich are generally very rich; *afraid to stir lest the*

insist upon the insertion into the Constitution of certain clauses which made it a contradiction to itself.[1] It was this which led them also to refuse, as we shall presently show, that all the public territory should be for ever free territory. The only question which has at any time seriously endangered the maintenance of the Union, has been that of slavery.[2] It was the determination to uphold and extend slavery, which impelled the South to demand the admission into the Union, as slave States, of Missouri, in 1818–20, and of California in 1848–50; in both these instances civil war was averted only by compromise measures, the North yielding a certain portion of its rights in both. In short, slavery has been, ever since 1820, the most serious question in the domestic politics of the United States, and it has influenced, directly and indirectly, the foreign policy of the Government more than any other.

It is perfectly evident, from the declarations of Southern journals and public men, and religious and political bodies, and from the manifestos of the seceding States themselves, that slavery, and nothing but slavery, has been the determining cause of the present civil war.

The Alabama Ordinance of Secession, for example, reads as follows:—[3]

"*Whereas*, the election of Abraham Lincoln and Hannibal Hamlin to the offices of President and Vice-President of the United States of America, by a sectional party avowedly hostile to the domestic institutions and the peace and security of the people of the State of Alabama, following upon the heels of many and dangerous infractions of the Constitution of the

---

British should burn their houses and carry off their negroes." (Helper's "Impending Crisis," p. 186.)

[1] In the discussions on the adoption of the Constitution, in 1787, it was from South Carolina that the proviso for the restoration of fugitive slaves came. And the delegates from the Carolinas and from Georgia declared unequivocally that if the slave-trade should be absolutely prohibited, as was at first intended, those States would not accept the Constitution, nor join the proposed Union. (Elliott's "Debates on the adoption of the Constitution.")

[2] The *Nullification* step of South Carolina was not really a serious danger to the Union, because that State stood alone; the slave States were opposed to her, and President Jackson, a slave-holder himself, took prompt and decided measures. But Jackson clearly saw through that attempt. He wrote of it, "The tariff was only the pretext, and disunion and a Southern Confederacy the real object. The next pretext will be the negro or slavery question." (Mr. Sumner's Speech.)

[3] Bacon's "Guide to American Politics," in which the Secession Ordinances of different States are reprinted.

United States, by many of the States and people of the Northern section, is a political wrong of so insulting and menacing a character as to justify the people of the State of Alabama in the adoption of prompt and decided measures for their future peace and security ;

Therefore, be it declared and ordained, by the people of the State of Alabama, in Convention assembled, that the State of Alabama now withdraws from the Union," &c. &c.

A letter addressed by the Presbyterian Synods at the South, " to all the Churches of the World," declares that " it is the antagonism between the South and the North on the subject of slavery which is at the root of all the difficulties that have brought about the rupture of the Union and the horrors of this unnatural war." [1]

The Rev. Dr. Palmer,[2] a distinguished Presbyterian divine of New Orleans, proclaimed from his pulpit, on the 29th Nov. 1860, the following sentiments: " In this great struggle we uphold the cause of God and religion. The spirit of abolitionism is unequivocally atheistical. Our mission is to preserve, and to transmit to posterity our system of slavery, and to obtain for it the right to go and take root wherever nature and Providence can transport it. . . . We cannot be satisfied with anything short of its extension. The position of the South at this moment is sublime. If she receive from God the grace to comprehend her mission, she will save herself by saving America and the world," &c.

The Bishops of the Protestant Episcopal Church of the South, in their Pastoral Letter of November 22, 1862, declared that the Confederate States, " having thrown off the hateful and infidel pestilence of abolitionism, are about to plant their national life on slavery."

The secular press of the South has been, if possible, even more explicit. We have already seen that one of its leading editors [3] has proclaimed, in an essay of great notoriety, that " the South is in the process of forming a slave republic." And after philosophising on the antagonistic difference of Northern and Southern societies, he adds, " Such, then, being the nature of the contest, the Union has been disrupted in the effort of slave society to emancipate itself."

1 " L'Amérique devant l'Europe," par M. de Gasparin.

2 London *Daily News*, August 8, 1863.

3 Mr. Spratt's " Essay on the Philosophy of Secession."

The Vice-President of the Confederacy[1] has boldly avowed the same truth in the following words:—

"Our new Constitution has put at rest for ever all the agitating questions relating to our peculiar institution, African slavery, as it exists among us—the proper status of the negro in our form of civilization. *This was the immediate cause of the late rupture and present revolution.* Jefferson, in his forecast, had anticipated this as 'the rock upon which the old Union would split.' He was right. . . . The foundations of our new Government are laid; its corner-stone rests upon the great truth that the negro is not equal to the white man; that slavery—subordination to the superior race—is his natural and moral condition. This our new Government is the first in the history of the world based upon this great physical, philosophical, and moral truth," &c. &c.

We also have a very strong corroborative evidence as to the real cause and object of Secession, in the fact that slavery is expressly recognised as a system, or "institution," and its extension provided for, in the Confederate Constitution. The Constitution of the United States terms slaves "*persons* held to service or labour;" the Constitution of the Confederate States calls them, plainly, "*slaves*" (Art. I. Sect. 2, Sect. 9; Art. IV. Sect. 2). The former nowhere recognises "the wild and guilty phantasy that man can hold property in man;" the latter expressly declares "the citizens of each State shall have the right of transit and sojourn in any State of this Confederacy with their *slaves and other property,* and *the right of property in such slaves* shall not thereby be impaired" (Art. IV. Sect. 2). The old Constitution makes no provision for the extension of slavery, but its whole spirit and intention are opposed to it, as were those of its most prominent framers, as we shall hereafter show; the Confederate Constitution proclaims that "the Confederate States may acquire new territory. In all such territory the institution of negro slavery, as it now exists in the Confederate States, shall be recognised and *protected by Congress and by the territorial governments, and the inhabitants of the several Confederate States and territories shall have the right to take to such territory any slaves lawfully held by them in any of the States or territories of the Confederate States*" (Art. IV. Sect. 3).[2]

If any additional evidence could be needed to establish the

[1] *Daily News*, Jan. 9, 1863.

[2] Bacon's "Guide to American Politics," pp. 61–81. A remarkable instance of the pertinacity with which the most notorious untruths are promulgated in England, concerning the parties to the War in America, was exhibited

true intent and purpose of Secession, we have it supplied to our hand by the Confederate Congress which, before adjourning in February, 1864, addressed to the Southern people a manifesto intended to encourage and stimulate them to prolonged resistance. This paper declares, "Compelled by a long series of oppressive and tyrannical acts" (which, we have proved, never were committed against the South, and which the Southern Vice-President himself utterly denied), "culminating at last in *the election of a President and Vice-President by a party confessedly sectional, and hostile to the South and her institutions,* these States withdrew from the former Union, and formed a new Confederate alliance, as an independent Government, *based on the proper relations of labour and capital,*" *i.e.* in which capital *owns* labour. It avows also that they "had a right to expect that they would be permitted, without molestation, to cultivate the arts of peace, *and vindicate in their chosen arena, and with the selected type of social characteristics,* their claims to civilization."

And now let us inquire, What had the United States' Government and the people of the North done, in the matter of slavery, to justify the South in this flagrant act of rebellion? Have they attempted to legislate upon the question of slavery in any of the Slave States? Never. The most violent haters of the "institution"—Garrison, the editor of the leading abolition journal in Boston, the various Emancipation and Abolition Societies at the North, the leaders of Anti-Slavery parties—have never dreamed of imposing upon the Slave States any

at a recent meeting of the Southern Independence Association, at Manchester. A report of the proceedings was published in the *Albion*, and reprinted in *Galignani's Messenger*, of Feb. 4, 1864. Mr. James Spence, the Financial Agent of the Confederacy, is reported to have made the following statement on that occasion, and we beg our readers to compare it with the above quotation: "The only bond which connects the States in the Southern Confederation is the Constitution, *which contains not a single principle in defence of slavery.*" Mr. Spence, moreover, made his speech after the chairman had commented on the comparative "*mendacity*" of the people of the Northern and Southern States and of England. He had appended the Confederate Constitution to his book on "The American Union," so that he must have been aware of its provisions. This is a fair sample of the undisguised partisan character of Mr. Spence's book. Those who have read, or may read it, should, in justice to the subject, consult some reliable commentary on the United States' Constitution, which will correct the mis-statements and inaccuracies, and supply the important omissions, made by the Financial Agent. Those who have not access to the classic works on the subject, will find a valuable epitome in Mr. Rawlins' little volume on "American Dis-Union," London, 1862: Robert Hardwicke.

legislative enactments upon the subject. All parties at the North were unanimous in the conviction that slavery was a municipal "institution" of the several States in which it existed; that it was not one of those matters concerning which the people had delegated to the General Government, under the Constitution, the power to legislate; and that, consequently, Congress should not even discuss the question of legislating upon slavery in the States. The Northern people did, unquestionably, desire and hope that the people of the Slave States themselves would see the evil which they were cherishing, and would themselves adopt some wise measures for removing it; their efforts were directed not to excite the slaves, but to enlighten the masters. This was a fundamental principle even of Mr. Garrison.

All that the Anti-Slavery men of the North asked or hoped for from Congress was, that laws should be enacted to exclude slavery from the public territories. Even this measure of justice, scant on every ground of humanity and wise policy (as will be made superabundantly evident, if it needed any proof), grew very slowly into anything like a general demand at the North, so unwilling were the people to give umbrage to their Southern brethren. In 1840, the Presidential Candidate of the Anti-Slavery Extension party received only 7,609 votes; in 1844, only 62,309 votes. In 1848, Mr. Van Buren, long the leader of the Democratic party, and who had been elected by it Vice-President, and subsequently President, of the United States, received, as the Presidential Candidate of the Anti-Slavery-Extension party, only 291,263 votes; though nominated by the delegates of all the Free States, as well as by those of Delaware, Maryland, Virginia, and the district of Columbia, he did not gain the electoral vote of a single State. Even in 1860, Mr. Lincoln did not receive the undivided support of the Northern people; in fact, he obtained only 300,000 more votes than his competitors combined. And what was the avowed determination of Mr. Lincoln and the Republican party which elected him? Simply, in the words of the Vice-President[1] of the Southern Confederacy, "to exclude slavery, by Acts of Congress, from the public territories, and *to oppose the extension of slavery* in every way." Now Mr. Lincoln was duly elected President, according to the forms prescribed by the Constitution; and

[1] Bigelow, "Les Etats-Unis en 1863," p. 143.

Congress, according to the same Constitution, has "power to dispose of and make all needful rules and regulations respecting the territory or other property belonging to the United States" (Art. IV. Sect. 3).

Thus the election of Mr. Lincoln to the Presidency of the Union inflicted no wrong upon the Slave States, and threatened none of the rights to which the Constitution entitled them. So far from it, they were solemnly assured by the man whom, a few months afterwards, they elected to be Vice-President of their own Confederacy, that, as they always had controlled the general Government, so they could continue to control it, if they chose to remain in the Union.[1]

From all the preceding considerations, we think that the following propositions are abundantly established:—1st. That the States possess no "Right of Secession" from the Union, other than the right of revolution; 2nd. That the Southern people had never either suffered, or been threatened with, any grievance from the United States Government, or from the people of the Free States, to justify their resort to this extremity; 3rd. That the rebellion was undertaken because the Southern leaders, finding that the extension of slavery was no longer possible in the Union, desired to found a new republic, based upon slavery, as "its corner-stone," and having the permanence and extension of slavery as its fundamental policy.

In the further consideration of our subject, therefore, we need only examine into the nature of this novel foundation for political institutions. We shall exhibit the real sentiments of the Southern people concerning their "peculiar institution," and their plans for its extension. We shall also endeavour to show some of the bad effects which slavery has already produced upon the South, by contrasting the moral and material condition of its population with that of the inhabitants of the Free States. Thus we shall be enabled to form some idea of the future career of the South as an independent "Slave Republic," and to determine whether or not the attempt to establish such a power should receive sanction or encouragement from humane Christian men, or civilized nations.

[1] *Ante*, p. 5.

I.

OPINIONS FORMERLY ENTERTAINED CONCERNING SLAVERY.

At the period of the War of Independence, slavery existed in all the English colonies which afterwards constituted the United States. But in those situated north of Virginia, the soil and climate, the distribution of land, and the agricultural products best adapted thereto, as well as the public sentiment, were all less favourable to slavery, as a system of labour, than in the Southern colonies. Consequently, it never had become so firmly rooted in the former as in the latter; and, during the twenty years which followed the war, slavery was more or less completely abolished in all the Northern States.

Southern writers, and amongst them the President of the Southern Confederacy, have endeavoured to prove that the Northern proprietors of slaves rid themselves of slavery by selling their slaves, or a great portion of them, to Southern planters. But there is no evidence whatever to show that this was the case, saving, perhaps, in a few exceptional instances.[1]

It was at the South, however, at that time, that the most earnest desires were expressed in favour of the abolition of the system of negro servitude, because it was there that the evils attending it were most felt. Washington, Jefferson, Madison, Henry, Randolph, Pinckney, Mason, Marshall, and others of the foremost men of the South, denounced the institution as severely as the most earnest Abolitionists of the present day can do.[2] They pointed out the danger to the community arising from the existence of so large a population, possessing no ties of interest

[1] Livermore, "Historical Research," Boston, 1863.

[2] Helper's "Impending Crisis at the South, and How to Meet it," chap. iii.

or of patriotism in common with the whites. Those men, too, who had been amongst the most prominent supporters of the Declaration of Independence, felt that it was a monstrous contradiction to profess "that all men are created equal; that they are endowed by their Creator with certain inalienable rights, among which are life, liberty, and the pursuit of happiness," while they denied those inalienable rights to hundreds of thousands of their fellow-creatures. The various social evils incident to the system were forcibly exhibited, in 1788, by Colonel Mason,[1] an ancestor of the late Confederate Commissioner to England:—"Slavery discourages arts and manufactures. The poor despise labour when performed by slaves. These prevent the immigration of whites, who really enrich and strengthen a country. They produce the most pernicious effect on manners. They bring the judgment of Heaven upon a country. As nations cannot be rewarded or punished in the next world, they must be in this. By an inevitable chain of causes and effects, Providence punishes national sins by national calamities."

At that early day, there was little or none of that antipathy to the negro, on account of his colour, which has so much prevailed since. Even in South Carolina, the Legislative Assembly,[2] in 1774, resolved, "That His Majesty's subjects in North America (without respect of colour or other accidents), are entitled to all the inherent rights and liberties of his natural-born subjects within the kingdom of Great Britain; that it is their fundamental right that no man should suffer in his person or property without a fair trial, and judgment given by his peers, or by the law of the land." By the original Articles of Confederation, it was declared that "the free inhabitants of each of these States (paupers, vagabonds, fugitives from justice, excepted) shall be entitled to all privileges and immunities of free citizens in the several States" (Art. IV). Thus free negroes were placed on the footing of citizenship with the whites. The delegates from South Carolina, indeed, demanded that citizenship should be restricted to the whites; but the demand was supported by the delegates from only two States, and it was rejected.[3] The Constitution, likewise, in the clause relating to taxation and representation

[1] Ibid. p. 165.
[2] Ibid. p. 186.
[3] Livermore, *op. cit.* pp. 25, 26.

(Art. I. Sect. 2), classes free negroes with whites; and another clause, as we have already pointed out, secures to all "the citizens of each State all the privileges and immunities of citizens in the several States," including free negroes.[1]

We have already said that the most prominent men in the Southern Colonies were desirous for the enfranchisement of the slaves. In the first Continental Congress, held in 1774, Mr. Jefferson,[2] as the organ of the delegates from Virginia, declared, "The abolition of domestic slavery is *the great object of desire* in these colonies." And as an essential initiatory step to this end an effort was made to stop the slave-trade. All the members of that Congress adopted and signed a series of articles to aid in the accomplishment of that purpose; and these articles were subsequently ratified by the Conventions of the different Southern States.[3] Those State Conventions were supported by unofficial popular meetings.[4]

Southerners of the olden time did not, as do their descendants of the present day, boldly affirm the right of property in man. In the Maryland Convention, in 1787-8, Mr. Pinckney[5] declared that "according to the natural and eternal principles of justice, no man has a right to hold a slave in bondage a single hour." Mr. Madison has recorded the fact that, "the idea that there could be a right of property in man was generally considered as monstrous, and that it should not be admitted into the Constitution." Hence the words *slave* and *slavery* were carefully excluded therefrom. Even that clause of the Constitution which relates to the restoration of fugitives "from service or labour," was sedulously weeded of the expression *servitude*, which was originally employed, and the word *service*[6] was, "on motion of Mr. Randolph, of Virginia, unanimously substituted; the former being thought to express the condition of slaves, the latter the obligation of free persons." Thus there is no clause in the Constitution of the United States which recognises slavery. It is the crowning distinction of the Southern Confederacy[7] that, in the nineteenth

1 See Note *ante*, p. 25.

2 Helper, *op. cit.* p. 154.

3 Livermore, *op. cit.* pp. 19, 20.

4 Helper, *op. cit.* p. 190.

5 Ibid. p. 172.

6 See "The Madison Papers," vol. iii. p. 1569.

7 See the extract from the Speech of Vice-President Stephens, and also the clauses quoted from the Confederate Constitution, on p. 33.

century, it should be "the first in the history of the world," not only to recognise and establish it, but to be avowedly and designedly founded upon it.

There is no way by which we can more surely prove the real meaning and intention of the Constitution, than by comparing its text with the sentiments, often and solemnly expressed, of its founders, or a majority of them. Judged in this manner, there is no doubt whatever that the Constitution did desire and intend that slavery should be gradually abolished,[1] and for this purpose two effectual measures, as it was thought at the time, were taken to prevent the increase and extension of the institution. These were, the exclusion of slavery from the larger portion of the public territories, and the limitation of the slave-trade to twenty years from the ratification of the Constitution. This is important to be kept in mind.

When the colonies declared their independence of Great Britain, most of them claimed extensive tracts of land to the west and north of the settlements, under their original charters. Dissensions and jealousies arose concerning them. But at the close of the war of Independence, certain of the States ceded to the general Government most of the unoccupied and partially-explored land which they severally owned, and it was hoped that all the States would do so. Foremost among the donors was Virginia. The public domain thus acquired was intended to constitute a common guarantee for the payment of the public debt contracted during the war. In 1784, under the old Articles of Confederation, a Committee of Congress, composed of three members, two of whom, including Mr. Jefferson, were from the South, proposed that from the whole of the actual and future public territory slavery should be for ever excluded after the year 1800. The delegates from the Carolinas and Georgia,

[1] The Vice-President of the Southern Confederacy has given his most valuable testimony to this fact. In his speech at Savannah, after the Secession, Mr. Stephens said: "The prevailing ideas entertained by Jefferson and most of the leading statesmen at the time of the formation of the old Constitution were, that the enslavement of the African was in violation of the laws of nature—that it was wrong in principle—socially, morally, and politically. It was an evil they knew not how to deal with; but the general opinion of the men of that day was that, somehow or other, in the order of Providence, the institution would be evanescent and pass away. This idea, though not incorporated in the Constitution, was the prevailing idea at the time."—London *Daily News*, Jan. 9, 1863.

together with one delegate from one other State, seven delegates in all, voted against this proposition. It was supported by all the delegates from six States, together with four others, in all sixteen votes. Nevertheless, this measure was lost, in consequence of the absence, on account of illness, of one of the delegates from New Jersey, who, however, was in favour of it; his colleague voted for it. The ballotting was by States, and not by delegates.

In 1787, a similar measure was passed, applicable only to that portion of the public territory lying north and west of the Ohio. The delegates from the Carolinas and Georgia voted in favour of this proposition. But they refused to consent that the territories which had belonged to them, and which were south of the Ohio, should be included in this law. Four Slave States have since been created out of this reserved territory, embracing 181,158 square miles.

It is important to bear in mind the intention of these two Bills, as they not only established a precedent for the disposition of the public lands, and showed that, in the estimation of the legislators of the day, Congress had a perfect right so to dispose of the public territory, but as they exhibit unmistakably the sentiments of the public men concerning the extension of slavery into the public territories.[1]

The history of the abolition of the slave-trade is as follows. In accordance with the opinions of the delegates to the Continental Congress of 1774, the African slave-trade had been partially prohibited by laws passed by the several State Assemblies, as we have already pointed out. In 1788, it was proposed, by an Article of the new Constitution, at once and for ever to abolish the trade. The delegates from all the Northern States, as well as those from Virginia, Maryland, and Delaware, were desirous that such an Article should be incorporated with the Constitution. But the delegates from the Carolinas and Georgia peremptorily declared that, if such a clause were introduced, those States would not enter into the proposed Union.[2] Accordingly,

[1] Ludlow's "History of the United States," pp. 46–48; Bigelow, "Les Etats-Unis en 1863," pp. 88–91.

[2] Livermore, *op. cit.* pp. 19, 20; also Mr. Sumner's "Speech on the Repeal of the Fugitive-Slave Law," p. 15. Mr. Stephens has also admitted the fact in his speech quoted on p. 4.

under this pressure, the Constitution was made to allow the slave-trade until 1808, the union of all the States being considered a matter of most vital and immediate necessity.

To-day, the advocates and apologists for slavery pretend that the relationship between masters and slaves is more or less similar to that between parents, or guardians, and minors; between tutors and pupils, between masters and apprentices. Judge Ruffin, of South Carolina,[1] thirty years ago, pronounced a very different opinion. He said, "The difference is that which exists between freedom and slavery, and a greater cannot be imagined. In the one, the end in view is the happiness of the youth born to equal rights with that governor or guide on whom the duty devolves of training the young to usefulness in a station which he is afterwards to assume among freemen. To such an end, and with such a subject, moral and intellectual instruction seem the natural means, and, for the most part, they are found to suffice. Moderate force is superadded only to make the other means effectual. With slavery it is far otherwise. The end is the profit of the master, his security, and the public safety; the subject is one doomed, in his own person and his posterity, to live without knowledge, and without the capacity to make anything his own, and to toil that another may reap the fruits. . . The power of the master must be absolute, to render the submission of the slave perfect."

Now we are told[2] that "slavery elevates the tone of the superior class, adds to its refinements, exalts the standard in morals, manners, and intellectual endowments," &c. &c. The Presbyterian Synod of South Carolina, thirty years ago, passed a different sentence upon the influence exerted by slavery upon the white population: "We have a mill-stone bound to our necks, which plunges us into an ocean of vice. Our children, from their earliest infancy, are corrupted by their contact with the slaves; and all our relations with them induce in ourselves an intellectual and moral deterioration."[3]

All over the Slave States the conviction was general, thirty

[1] Helper, *op. cit.* p. 179.

[2] Address on Climatology, before the New Orleans Academy of Science, by Dr. Barton, quoted by Mr. Olmsted, "Journeys and Explorations in the Cotton Kingdom," vol. ii. p. 277.

[3] "Les Etats-Unis en 1861," par M. le Pasteur Fisch, Paris, 1862; p. 199.

years ago, that they were retrograding as compared with the Free States; and a wave of public sentiment swelled high in Virginia, but died away as it reached South Carolina, to sweep away the curse from the land. Judge Gaston,[1] one of the most enlightened men of North Carolina, said, "Disguise it as we may, and throw the blame where we may, *it is slavery* which, more than any other cause, keeps us back in the career of improvement. It stifles industry and represses enterprise; it is fatal to economy and prudence; it discourages skill, impairs our strength as a community, and poisons morals at the fountain-head." During the discussions in the Virginia Legislature, in 1832, the last time that a vigorous effort was made to abolish slavery in that State, when the enormities and evils of the system were thoroughly exposed by many able men, Mr. Faulkner, late United States minister to France, summed up his bill of indictment against it as follows:—

"If there be one who believes in the harmless character of this institution, let me request him to compare the condition of the slave-holding portion of this commonwealth—barren, desolate, and scarred, as it were, by the avenging hand of Heaven—with the descriptions we have of this country from those who first broke its soil. To what is this change ascribable? *Alone to the withering and blasting effects of slavery.* If this does not satisfy him, let me request him to extend his travels to the Northern States of this Union, and contrast the happiness and contentment which prevail throughout that country—the busy and cheerful sounds of industry, the rapid growth of their population, their means and institutions of education, their skill and proficiency in the useful arts, their enterprise and public spirit, the monuments of their commercial and manufacturing industry, and, above all, their devoted attachment to the Government from which they derive their protection—*with the division, discontent, indolence, and poverty of the Southern country.* To what, sir, is all this ascribable? To that vice in the organization of society by which one-half of the inhabitants are arrayed in feeling and interest against the other half; to that unfortunate state of society in which free men regard labour as disgraceful, and slaves shrink from it as a burden tyrannically imposed upon them; to that condition of things in which half a million of your population can feel no sympathy with the society in the prosperity of which they are forbidden to participate, and no attachment to a Government at whose hands they receive nothing but injustice. . . . Does the slaveholder, while he is enjoying his slaves, reflect upon the deep injury and incalculable loss the possession of that property inflicts upon the

[1] Address before the Literary Societies of the University of North Carolina. Helper, *op. cit.* p. 181.

country? Slavery, it is admitted, is an evil; it is an institution which presses heavily upon the best interests of the State. It banishes free white labour; it exterminates the mechanic, the artisan, the manufacturer. It deprives them of occupation. It deprives them of bread. It converts the energy of a community into indolence, its power into imbecility, its efficiency into weakness. Sir, as it is thus injurious, have we not a right to demand its extermination? Shall society suffer, that the slave-holder may continue to gather his crop of human flesh? What is his mere pecuniary claim compared with the great interests of the common weal? Must the country languish, droop, die, that the slave-holder may flourish? Shall all interests be subservient to one—all rights subordinate to those of the slave-holder? Have not the middle classes their rights—rights incompatible with the existence of slavery?"[1]

An effort was made in Kentucky, even so late as 1848, by Mr. Clay, to provide for the abolition of slavery by introducing into the amended Constitution of that State the requisite powers; but the effort failed there, as elsewhere, and from causes which we shall presently explain.

[1] Helper, *op. cit.* p. 86 and p. 140.

II.

CHANGE OF SENTIMENT AT THE SOUTH.

Gradually, during the last thirty years or more, a complete revolution has taken place in Southern sentiment, under the guidance especially of Mr. Calhoun and his fellow-citizens of South Carolina.

About thirty years ago, Mr. Calhoun made the discovery that "Slavery is the surest and most solid foundation in the world for free institutions." Governor M'Duffie, of the same State, varied the peal a little, by announcing that "Slavery is the very corner-stone of our Republican edifice." Governor Hammond, of the same State, completed the chime, and rang out, "Slavery is not only a necessary and inexorable fact, but it is a moral and humane institution, productive of the greatest political and social advantages."

It was natural that so all-engrossing a question should have extended into religious bodies. One after another, most of the various religious sects in the United States became divided thereby, those of the South separating from their Northern brethren. And it is important to note that, in the different manifestoes issued from time to time by the former, to explain their schismatic proceedings, *they have uniformly borne witness to the opposition which slavery has met with at the North.* This is a precious admission, inasmuch as now it is pretended, by Southerners and by their English friends, that the North is not opposed to slavery, and that this institution is more likely to cease under Southern independence, by voluntary abolition, than it will under Northern supremacy, that is, under a renewed Union.

In the Letter[1] addressed by the Presbyterian Synods of the

[1] "L'Amérique devant l'Europe," par M. de Gasparin. We have already quoted another sentence from this Letter, p. 32.

South "to all the Churches on Earth," it is stated to be "certain that the North cherishes a profound antipathy against slavery, whilst the South is animated with a zeal equally strong in favour of that institution."

The Rev. Dr. Palmer,[1] of New Orleans, said, in the sermon from which we have already quoted, "It cannot be denied that the population of the North is almost without exception opposed to slavery, if it be not actually Abolitionist. The whole of the present generation there has been brought up to hate it as a national sin. There they hope and expect and pray that it may be abolished within a reasonable time; and they cannot be satisfied unless they see that some progress is being made towards this end. We, on the other hand, chosen guardians of slavery, we cannot be satisfied with anything less than its extension," &c.

On the 22nd November, 1862, the Bishops of the Protestant Episcopal Church of the Southern States addressed a Pastoral Letter to their flocks. In this letter a commendable desire is manifested to aid in reforming the abuses which the Bishops deplore as being rife at the South on the subject of slavery—abuses which the Bishops charge in great part upon the clergy. They declare that *the Church at the South is unanimous in the support of slavery.* They admit the gross ignorance which prevails, and exhort the clergy to "strip themselves of their pride and fastidiousness and indolence," and devote themselves zealously to give to the slaves "that religious and moral instruction which is to elevate them in the scale of being." (p. 11.) They then speak of "the duty of the Church to press upon the masters of the country their obligations as Christians so to arrange this institution as not to *necessitate* the violation of those sacred relations which God has created, and which man cannot, consistently with Christian duty, annul. The systems of labour which prevail in Europe," they continue, "and which are in many respects more severe than ours, are so arranged as to prevent all necessity for the separation of parents and children, and of husbands and wives; and a very little care on our part would rid *the system upon which we are about to plant our national life* of those unchristian features. . . . Hitherto we have been hindered by the pressure of Abolitionism; *now that we have thrown off from us that hateful and infidel pestilence* we should prove to the world that we are

[1] London *Daily News*, Aug. 8, 1863; also *ante*, p. 32.

faithful to our trust," &c. &c. (p. 12.) What more complete acknowledgment of the existence of two of the greatest evils attendant upon slavery, the utter disregard of the social ties and relations of the slaves, and the absence of any systematic moral and religious and intellectual training, could be given? And what more complete evidence of the determination of the religious leaders of the people to have nothing to do with *abolition* could the Southern Independence Association in England desire?[1]

More recently still a manifesto, signed by a hundred clergymen, Presbyterians, Episcopalians, Baptists, Methodists, &c., has been addressed "to Christians throughout the World;" extraordinary efforts were made to circulate it widely throughout Great Britain.[2] This paper declares that "surrounded as we are with all the facts bearing upon slavery, and knowing well its practical operation, we solemnly testify before God that the relationship between the master and the slave, as it exists here, is not incompatible with our holy Christianity, notwithstanding the many abuses which we deplore, and which exist also in other human relations. The existence of Africans in our country gives us reason to bless God on their account. The condition of the slaves is not wretched, as Northern writers of fiction would have us believe, but it is prosperous and happy; and it would have been much more so if the false zeal of the Abolitionists had not prevented us. . . . We consider Abolitionism is an obstacle to the plans of God. It does not bear the mark of the Lord's blessing. It is a fanaticism which produces no good fruit."

It is strange that Christians, seeing how utterly neglected the religious instruction of the slaves has always been, should pretend that one of the advantages of slavery is that *it christianizes the African.* Yet this is one of the arguments urged not only in favour of slavery, but also of re-opening the African slave-trade. The Rev. Dr. Thornwall,[3] said to be one of the most distinguished theologians of South Carolina, has expressed his conviction that "*The slave-trade is the most worthy of all the Missionary Societies.*"

1 Pastoral Letter from the Bishops of the Protestant Episcopal Church to the Clergy and Laity of the Church in the Confederate States of America. Delivered before the General Council, in St. Paul's Church, Augusta, Saturday, Nov. 22, 1862.

2 London *Daily News*, Aug. 8, 1863.

3 "Les Etats-Unis en 1863," par M. le Pasteur Fisch, p. 189.

In fact, the opinions which have been everywhere avowed, during the last few years, by the most intelligent people of the South, as to the excellence of the "institution," are more like the ravings of delirium than the sober expressions of sensible men. Thus *The Southern Literary Messenger*, of Charleston, the oldest and the most widely read of all the Southern periodicals,[1] recently favoured the world with the following definition: "*An Abolitionist* is a man who does not love slavery for its own sake, as a divine institution; who does not worship it as a corner-stone of civil liberty; who does not adore it as the only possible social condition, on which a permanent Republican Government can be erected; and who does not, in his inmost soul, desire to see it extended and perpetuated over the whole earth, as a means of human reformation, *second only in dignity, importance and sacredness to the Christian religion itself.*"

Mr. Fitzhugh, of Virginia,[2] in a book on the "Sociology of the South," says: "The Jewish slaves were not negroes, and to confine the justification of slavery to the negro race would be to weaken the scriptural authority and to lose the weight of profane authority; for we read of no negro slavery in ancient times. Slavery, black or white, is right and necessary."

The Richmond Enquirer,[3] the most authoritative, perhaps, of the Southern journals, declares "Repeatedly have we asked the North—'Has not the experiment of universal liberty failed? Are not the evils of free society insufferable?' Still no answer. Their silence is a conclusive proof, added to many others we have furnished, that free society, in the long run, is an impracticable form of society: it is everywhere starving, demoralized, and insurrectionary. Policy and humanity alike forbid the extension of the evils of free society to new people and coming generations. Until recently the apologists of slavery took half-way grounds. They confined the defence of slavery to negro slavery, thereby giving up the *principle* of slavery, admitting other forms of servitude to be wrong. The South now maintains that slavery of itself is right, natural, and necessary. While it is far more obvious that negroes should be slaves rather than whites—for they are only fit to labour, not to direct—yet

[1] Quoted by Professor Cairnes, "The Slave Power," p. 177.

[2] London *Daily News*, March 19, 1863.

[3] Ibid.

the principle of slavery is itself right, and does not depend upon complexion."

Another Virginian journal,[1] *The Southside Democrat,* admits, "We have got to hating everything with the prefix *free,* from free negroes up and down the whole catalogue—free farms, free labour, free society, free will, free thought, and free schools. But the worst of all these abominations is free schools." The article then discusses the best way of disposing of those poor people who are not able to educate their children; and concludes, "Let our Legislature pass a law, that whoever will take these parents, and take care of them and their offspring in health and sickness, clothe them, feed them, and house them, shall be legally entitled to their services."

These sentiments are not intended to be idle talk. We shall see, from the career and condition of the Slave States, that they have been, and are meant still to be, the controlling policy of that section, so long as they can be carried out.

And now, how is this great change which has come over the Southern mind, since the era of Washington and his contemporaries, to be accounted for?

The clergy of the South, as we have seen, ascribe it to Northern Abolitionism. And this explanation generally passes current at the South, and is re-echoed by the friends of slavery everywhere. But nothing can be more untrue.

We have seen that, so long ago as the Declaration of Independence, the prominent statesmen of the South saw and deplored the same evils which the Southern Bishops now acknowledge to be chargeable to Slavery. Then the ignorance, the gross immorality, the idleness, the general impoverishment of the whites at the South, were charged upon slavery by slaveholders, and were urged, not only upon State Legislatures, but upon the General Government, as convincing arguments for the necessity of abolition. The great men of the South were then Abolitionists in the best sense of the term; and there was not a man or a woman at the South, possessed of brains or heart, who would not have despised or pitied the author of the definition of *an Abolitionist,* which we have quoted from the pink of Southern reviews. So lately as 1832, nowhere at the North could

[1] London *Daily News,* March 19, 1863.

slavery have been more bitterly and more truly denounced than it was in Southern legislative halls.[1] In 1830, of the thirty-six Abolition Societies which existed in the United States, *twenty-eight* were established in the Slave States. One of these, "The Virginia Society for the Abolition of Slavery," established in 1791, addressed a memorial to Congress,[2] in which it testified "that slavery is not only an odious degradation, but an outrageous violation of one of the most essential rights of human nature, and utterly repugnant to the precepts of the Gospel," &c. A pamphlet published[3] under the auspices of the "Manumission Society of North Carolina," in 1830, calls upon "the friends of virtue, humanity, patriotism, and, above all, religion, to awaken to a sense of the many principles of injustice, inhumanity, and irreligion which attend our system of African slavery. . . . We have impartially examined the evil in its origin, its progress, and its present state, as well as its future consequences; and, even in its mildest form, it shrinks from rational inspection—*a monster of hideous deformity in its best feature*." At that time, the only special Abolition journal in the United States was published in the slave-holding city of Baltimore.[4] It was not until after this period, and then only in consequence of the constant and unscrupulous aggressions of the South upon the intent and letter of the Constitution, that the spirit, not of Abolitionism, but of opposition to the extension of slavery, began to show itself at the North. We have already indicated how gradually and how *unaggressively* that spirit manifested itself.[5] In fact, during the first years of his career as editor and publisher of *The Liberator*, in Boston, Mr. Garrison was scarcely tolerated; his establishment was destroyed, and he himself was imprisoned; and the term *Abolitionist* was one of reproach. It is only *within three years* that Garrison, Wendell Phillips, Sumner, and other avowed Abolitionists have been able to speak to public audiences, universally, in the Northern cities. At Washington, the South was all-powerful, so as to prevent the reception, by the House of Representatives, of the most respectful Petitions in favour of

[1] See *ante*, p. 43.
[2] Helper, *op. cit.* p. 173.
[3] Ibid. p. 183.
[4] Ludlow's "History of the United States," p. 166; "Les Etats-Unis en 1863."
[5] *Ante*, pp. 34-36.

abolishing slavery in the district of Columbia, and even "all memorials, petitions, resolutions, or propositions *having any reference to slavery.*" This rule was not abrogated until 1845, during ten years.[1]

No! The charge of Abolitionism made against the North never had any foundation. The North was too unwilling to occasion sectional animosity, too unwilling to give the South any "occasion of offence," even at the expense of justice and humanity. The charge was made by the slaveholders, aware of its untruth, in order to unite the Southern people against the North, that by intimidation the latter should be forced to concede everything to ensure the extension of slavery.

Mr. Calhoun, having failed to unite the South on the Tariff question, raised the cry of *Abolitionism.* He established a journal at Washington, *The United States Telegraph,* in order to advocate the special policy of the South. Mr. Hill, Senator from New Hampshire, a Democrat and an ally of the South, protested, in the Senate, that he "abhorred the Abolitionists," but that not all their publications and other efforts combined could do one-half the mischief which was being accomplished by this single journal of Mr. Calhoun.[2] Ex-President Madison, a slaveholder, writing to Mr. Clay, also a slaveholder, said, "It is painful to see the unceasing efforts made to alarm the South, by imputations against the North of unconstitutional designs on the subject of slavery." To another, he wrote, "The inculcated impression of a permanent incompatability of interests between the North and the South may put it in the power of *popular leaders, aspiring to the highest stations,* to unite the South on some critical occasion. In pursuing this course, the first and most obvious step is nullification, the next secession, and the last a final separation."[3]

[1] "Les Etats-Unis en 1863," p. 143.

[2] Ludlow, *op. cit.* pp. 164, 165.

[3] Ibid. The slaves have, undoubtedly, been indebted to their masters for the knowledge that they must look to the North for friends and freedom. No restraint whatever seems to have been placed upon the whites in exaggerating the efforts made by Northern Abolitionists in behalf of the negroes. At public meetings, at elections, at social entertainments, in ordinary fire-side converse, slaves being present, and hearing all, or enough, the opposition of the North to slavery has been the great topic of speech-making and of talk. This has been particularly the case at the epochs of Presidential elections. Thus the slaves

But what had the Southerners to fear from Northern Abolitionists? Not, surely, that the latter would go to the plantations, and preach insurrection to the slaves. If any man, fool enough to undertake such an errand, had been found in any Slave State, he would have been hung on the nearest tree. Not that any abolition publication would have been circulated amongst the slaves. In the first place, Northern Abolitionists did not address themselves to the slaves, but to the masters, in their publications; and secondly, not one slave in a hundred thousand could have read them, no matter how incendiary they might have been. Mr. Calhoun's journal made known the danger which the slave-owners foresaw: "The real danger of a slave-insurrection is remote. We have most to fear from the organized action upon the consciences and fears of slaveholders themselves—from the insinuation of their dangerous heresies into our schools, our pulpits, and our domestic circles. It is only by alarming the consciences of the weak, and by diffusing amongst our people a morbid sensibility on the question of slavery, that the Abolitionists can accomplish anything."[1] "Conscience makes cowards of us all." It was the enlightenment of their own consciences by the truth which the slave-owners were most anxious to avoid.

The true explanation of the change of sentiment is not to be

have been made aware, not by Abolitionists, but by Southerners themselves, that a political ferment was going on, in which they were the persons most interested. The candidateship of Fremont, and the apprehensions entertained at the South of his success, must have been in this way quite well known amongst the slaves, especially amongst the house-servants, from whom the facts, exaggerated and diversely interpreted, would spread to the field-hands. But the extraordinary importance of the last Presidential election, upon the result of which so much was known to depend, must have been the subject of constant thought and conversation amongst the negroes; and they must have looked forward to its decision as to the cardinal point of their fate. Knowing, too, that a great political party was formed for the especial object of limiting slavery, and gradually bringing it to an end, they could well bide their time. Probably this reflection has contributed very much to the non-occurence of insurrections amongst them, which everyone looked upon as one of the certainties of the war. It is curious to note the idea which the slaves have of Mr. Lincoln. In the "Report of the Commission on the Condition of the Freedmen," a conversation amongst some freed slaves at Hilton Head is alluded to, which a grey-headed *sachem* of the party interruped as follows: "Massa Linkum! what you know 'bout Massa Linkum Massa Linkum eb'ry whar; he walk de erf like de Lord!"

[1] Olmsted's "Journeys and Explorations," vol. ii. p. 357.

found, then, in any fancied danger of slave-insurrection, excited by Northern Abolitionists. It exists in that baser motive which underlies the whole system of slavery—"*the ignoble love of gold.*" Nowhere, perhaps, more strongly than in the origin and extension of slavery, is it apparent that "the love of money is the root of all evil." The enormous expansion of the cotton-crop of the South, and, to a less degree, that of rice, tobacco, and sugar, explains the whole mystery.

The agricultural history of the Slave States proves that, under the system of slave labour, they have been undergoing a constant and progressive deterioration in comparative productiveness, and in the value of land. Slave labour necessitates simplicity of agricultural operations, on account of the ignorance of the labourers and their want of interest in the result of their toil. In the Northern range of Slave States, tobacco has always been almost the only product cultivated for sale; in the Southern States, cotton.

From of old, Virginia had the monopoly of tobacco. It was the great standard of value for every thing. A clergyman's salary was fixed by law at 16,000 pounds of tobacco, with perquisites, as 200 pounds of tobacco for a marriage service, and 400 pounds of the same weed for a funeral sermon. It was the only article which could be sold, and therefore every one cultivated it. Even so late as the time of the Revolutionary war, the tobacco-crop of Virginia was worth twice as much as all the other agricultural products of the colony, and ten times as much as all the shipping, timber, naval-stores, peltry, and other productions of the forest, fisheries, mines, and manufactures.[1] So long as the foreign slave-trade existed, under the auspices of the mother-country, the annual increase of labourers, amounting to about 1,000[2] in 1724, permitted of an aggregate augmentation of the crop, in spite of the diminishing fertility of

[1] Olmsted's "Seaboard Slave States," pp. 242, 271. Beverley, in the early part of the last century, chronicled the fact that the colonists of Virginia were repeatedly menaced with famine from their neglecting to plant corn enough for themselves, that they might sow more tobacco. And, until a comparatively late period, the colonists were frequently stimulated by laws to plant more corn and less tobacco, just as the people of the Southern States, during the last three years, have been often reminded by their legislators to neglect cotton-planting in favour of cereals.

[2] Ibid. p. 238.

the soil. But the demand did not increase in proportion to the supply; prices fell, and the planters were steadily becoming impoverished, notwithstanding repeated attempts, by legislative enactments, to limit production and force prices. Property was, before the Revolution, much more unequally divided than it has been since the laws of primogeniture and descent in tail were repealed. So early as 1677, the English proprietaries of the colony [1] upbraided the colonists for "the lazy rapacity with which each desired to surround himself with a large expanse of property, over which he could exert no other act of ownership than that of excluding the occupants by whom it might be advantageously cultivated." The same disposition continued, under the combined influence of impoverishment of soil, low prices of products, and fresh importations of slaves. But at the time of the Revolution, "the average property of a majority of the able-bodied, tax-paying men in Virginia was less than one hundred dollars." [2] The condition into which the landed proprietors had gradually fallen is thus described by a Virginian, in the *Southern Planter*. "Every farm was greatly impoverished — almost every estate was seriously impaired — some were involved in debt to nearly their value. . . . No farm, whether of a rich or a poor proprietor, had escaped great exhaustion. . . . Every one was desirous to sell his land, and move to the fertile and far West, and a general emigration and dispersion were only prevented by the impossibility of finding purchasers for the lands, even at half the then low market prices." [3] In 1832, a member of the State Legislature [4] declared that, "In that part of the State situated on the rivers below tide-water, the whole face of the country wears an appearance of utter desolation. The very spot on which our ancestors landed, two hundred years ago, appears to be on the point of again becoming the haunt of wild beasts." It was in the midst of these discouraging circumstances, that a new pursuit was opened to recruit the finances and enkindle the hopes of the agriculturists of Virginia —*the breeding of slaves for Southern cotton fields.*

Slavery had produced the same results in the Carolinas and

[1] Olmsted's "Seaboard Slave States," p. 250.

[2] Ibid. p. 267.

[3] Ibid. p. 274.

[4] Helper, *op. cit.* p. 88. See also Mr. Faulkner's speech, *ante*, p. 43.

Georgia as in Virginia; the general poverty was perhaps even greater there than in Virginia, because they had no agricultural monopoly of the same importance as tobacco. But, in the beginning of the present century, the prospects of those States brightened under the growing demand for *Cotton.*

Until about the close of the Revolutionary war, the cotton-plant had been cultivated only as an ornament to gardens. In 1784, according to Mr. De Bow, *eight bales* of cotton, which had been shipped from America, were seized at the English Custom House, under the belief that so large a quantity could not have come from that source. In 1790, the exportation was only eighty-one bales.[1] But, at about this period, improved machinery was invented in England and America for cleaning and weaving cotton, so that the demand for it increased amazingly. In 1794, the cotton-crop was valued at $500,000; in 1800, at $5,000,000. It was evident, however, that this growing demand could only be supplied by increasing the number of slaves; for then, as ever since, the whites would not work in the cotton-fields. But, in 1774-5, the colonies, as we have seen, had agreed to discourage the foreign slave-trade, the Carolinas and Georgia as well as the others. In 1787-8, these colonies, or rather States, refused to allow a clause absolutely and at once prohibiting the traffic in slaves to be introduced into the new Constitution, and thus the trade was left open for twenty years. South Carolina did, from year to year, prohibit her own citizens engaging in it, until 1804, from which time until 1808 it was unrestricted; and during those four years, no less than 35,532[2] Africans were introduced into the port of Charleston alone. Most, if not all, the other

[1] Bigelow, *op. cit.* p. 370.

[2] The author of a pamphlet, "La Révolution Américaine dévoilée," Paris, 1861, seems to think that the people of the Slave States had a much greater aversion to the slave-trade than any other people; and yet, according to his own statement, about *one-eleventh* of the whole number of slaves introduced into Charleston were introduced by Southerners (3,543), while the entire white population of the Slave States, at the period in question, could not have been over one million, which was a small fractional part of the population of Great Britain, France, Holland, and the Northern States of America, which were likewise engaged in the slave-trade. Again, the commercial tonnage of the South was utterly insignificant as compared with that of these others combined, or of any one of them. The same writer mentions, with great satisfaction, that the consignees of the slavers were—natives of Charleston, 13; of the North, 88; of Great Britain, 91; of France, 10; total, 202: and these figures, he thinks,

States did interdict the slave-trade to their own citizens previous to the year 1808, at which time the prohibition of the Constitution took effect. Subsequently to this period, the cotton planters became dependent upon the Northern Slave States for fresh slaves, over and above the supply afforded by the natural increase of their own black populations. And as the demand for cotton grew with immense rapidity, and as new Slave States were being added to the Union, in which cotton was the great staple of production, this natural increase of the slave population by no means kept pace with the necessities of the planters.

The only source whence the needed slaves could be obtained was the Northern Border Slave States, and especially Virginia. The temptation thus presented was too strong to be resisted. Slavery, which had begun to be looked upon as a dreadful evil that must be thrown off, not only for its moral influences, but for the enormous expense and loss it entailed, now resumed its hold upon the planters as a means of retrieving their fortunes. Legitimate agriculture, which, under the example of a few intelligent farmers, was beginning to improve in character, was comparatively abandoned; land became of less importance than slaves; and, in consequence of the high price of labour, improvements of all sorts, of a public nature, and all industrial pursuits, have been more and more neglected, to the great detriment of the State.[1]

The number of slaves annually sold from the Border States to the cotton-growing States is very large. In 1857 a Committee of the Legislature of South Carolina reported that, from 1840 to 1850, no less than 235,000 slaves had been obtained from this source, most of them being able-bodied and in the prime of life; Of these nearly one-half came from Virginia. Estimating each of these as worth from five hundred to seven hundred dollars, we have the apparent profit which the *breeding States* have derived from this novel industry. And this is almost the sole profit which they, and especially Virginia, have, for years past, obtained

prove the comparative detestation in which the Charlestonians held this traffic. But Charleston, at that period, 1804–1808, contained only 20,000 inhabitants, with a very small amount of shipping; yet it furnished almost *one-fifteenth* part of all the consignees of the slave cargoes.

[1] Olmsted's "Seaboard Slave States," *loc. cit.*

from slavery. Mr. Clay[1] said, in 1829, "Nowhere in the *farming* portion of the United States would slave-labour be generally employed, if the proprietors were not tempted to raise slaves to sell, by the high price paid for them in the cotton-growing States." Judge Upshur, of Virginia, stated at a Convention, that a law passed in Louisiana, in 1829, interposing obstacles to the introduction of slaves into that State, caused a decline of 25 per cent. in the value of slaves in Virginia. Governor Wise declared that the failure to secure the admission of California as a Slave State, in 1850, occasioned a loss to Virginia of $4,000 for each able-bodied negro she possessed.[2]

The increasing value of slave property was an argument used in the Legislature of Virginia, in 1832, against abolition. Mr. Gholson contended that slave-owners were as much entitled to the annual profit on their female slaves, as the owners of land, or the owners of orchards, to the annual increase from these. "It is in reliance on the justice and inviolability of this maxim," said he, "that the master foregoes the service of the female slave, has her nursed and attended during the period of gestation, and raises the helpless offspring. The value of the property justifies the expense; and I do not hesitate to say, that its increase constitutes much of our wealth."[3]

Thus the true reason why the people of the Slave States to-day

[1] Helper, *op. cit.* p. 163.

[2] Cairnes, *op. cit.* pp. 127–137. It might have been supposable, *à priori*, that, under such a drain as this, slavery would be exhausted in the breeding States. In fact it was said this would prove to be the case by those who wished, at the origin of the internal slave-trade, to discover some compensating good for that which instinctively struck everyone as an unmitigated enormity, worse even than the foreign slave-trade. But the reverse has been the case. From 1790 to 1800, the slave-population of Virginia increased 17·84 per cent. ; from 1810 to 1820, only 8·31 per cent. ; so that slavery seemed to be dying a natural death. But Missouri was admitted as a Slave State in 1820, and from 1820 to 1830 the slave population of Virginia had increased 10·49 per cent. From 1830 to 1840 the rate of increase was smaller again, 4·40 per cent. ; but Texas was admitted into the Union as a Slave State in 1845, and the slave population of Virginia increased at the rate of 5·21 per cent. from 1840 to 1850 (United States' Census Report, 1860). The reason of this seeming paradox is simple. Slaves in Virginia being prized, more than formerly, as *breeders* rather than as labourers, are better cared for, better fed, and not hardly worked. In 1860, the slaves in Virginia, instead of having diminished since 1850, under the drain of the internal slave-trade, which carried off not less than 10,000 yearly, had increased by 28,337.

[3] Olmsted, *op. cit.* p. 282. Mr. Ruffin, of Virginia, says that "a gang of

think so differently of slavery from their fathers is, simply, that the institution pays a better percentage than it did sixty years ago. The production and sale of cotton, and the production and sale of slaves have apparently retarded the ruin of Virginia and the Carolinas, only to make that ruin ultimately more wide-spread and more complete; an additional few have been enriched at the expense of additional millions who have been made each year more poor and more wretched by the prolongation of slavery. It has not been, then, *the fanaticism* of Northern Abolitionists, but "*the ignoble love of gold*" of the planters and slave-dealers; it has not been any improvement in the nature and results of the system, but "*the greed of wealth*" obtainable therefrom, which has so changed its whole aspect in the estimation of Southern statesmen, and has induced them to make it "the corner-stone" of their new political fabric.

slaves on a farm will increase to four times their original number in thirty or forty years. If a farmer is only able to feed and maintain his slaves, their increase in value may double the whole of his capital originally invested in farming, before he closes the term of an ordinary life. But few farms are able to support this increasing expense, and also to furnish the necessary supplies to the family of the owner; whence *very many owners of large estates in lands and negroes are, throughout their lives, too poor to enjoy the comforts of life,* or to incur the expenses necessary to improve their unprofitable farming. . . . The income of few persons increases as fast as their slaves; and, if not, the consequence must be that some of them will be sold to support the rest; and the sale of more is, perhaps, afterwards compelled, to pay debts incurred in striving to put off that dreaded alternative. The slave at first almost starves his master, and at last is eaten by him—at least, is exchanged for his value in food" (*Ibid.* p. 280). What a picture of the Virginia *Aristocracy!* Thus even this new source of wealth is a fallacious one. It was right that such a cursed source of gain should ruin its pursuers. Actæon was devoured by his own hounds.

III.

THE ENCROACHMENTS OF SLAVERY.

HAVING become convinced by their cupidity that "slavery[1] is a great moral, social, and political blessing—a blessing to the slave, and a blessing to the master," the leading men of the South have devoted themselves, for the last forty years or more, to perpetuate the system. And herein consists the great folly and crime of the South, and, to a less extent, of the whole United States. Slavery had been entailed upon the colonies by Great Britain,[2] for the sake of the gains derived from the African slave-trade. The colonies had declared, as one of their grievances against the King and Government of England, that their repeated efforts to prevent this traffic had been invariably "defeated by His Majesty's negative." Yet after they had abjured the Royal authority, they themselves deliberately re-instated the African slave-trade, which they had, for a short time, prohibited. And not content with increasing their slave-population, the cotton-growing States had refused to exclude slavery from all the public territory, and had reserved more than 180,000 square miles of it for the extension of the institution.[3]

The continued extension of slavery over new territories could only be accomplished by the Slave States acquiring and maintaining political supremacy in national affairs. It was necessary that they should possess in the United States' Senate, to which each State sends two delegates, if not an actual majority of votes, at least a minority large enough to prevent any legislation hostile to their policy. They could not hope to retain a majority

[1] Senator Brown, of Mississippi, quoted by Mr. Sumner in his "Speech on the Barbarism of Slavery," p. 7.

[2] See the Stipulations of the Treaty of Utrecht.

[3] *Ante*, p. 41.

in the House of Representatives, because the population of the Free States, increasing much more rapidly than that of the Slave States, determined the political complexion of that Chamber. But the assent of the Senate was necessary to the enactment of all important laws.

From the adoption of the Constitution until 1819, the question of slavery was in abeyance. Four new States, formed out of the territory ceded to the General Government in 1787, and from which slavery was excluded by the act of cession, were successively admitted as Free States; and four others, formed out of the territory reserved by the Carolinas and Georgia, were received as Slave States, together with Louisiana, a portion of the territory purchased from France, and in which slavery was allowed in virtue of the treaty of purchase. Thus, in 1819, the Union was composed of eleven States of each category.

Since that time the history of the two sections is but a recital of perpetual conflicts on the slavery question,—the South boldly advancing upon the North as timidly retreating. The reason of this is twofold. The South, since 1820, has been always united upon this all-engrossing interest, while the North has been divided by conflicting questions of commerce, agriculture, manufactures, &c. However severed, at times, on the Bank question, on the Tariff policy, on the subject of internal improvements by the National Government, &c., &c., the cry of *Slavery* has rallied all the Southern forces around the black banner, and has recruited these largely from Northern mercenaries, hungry for the spoils of victory. Again, the *patriotism* of the Northern people has not been hemmed in by narrow State limits. While the Southerner has been devoted to Virginia, or Carolina, or Tennessee, the Northern man has held to the grand Union of all the States, as the palladium of prosperity and safety.

It has been to preserve domestic peace, and this Union one and indivisible, into which, as they firmly believe, the hopes of liberal men all over the world have been garnered, that the Northern people have yielded to the wild and incendiary threats of Southern slaveholders, until further yielding had become impossible.

It will not be necessary for us to recount the various steps of Southern aggressions on freedom and free territory—accompanied always by threats of bloodshed, civil war, and disunion, whenever those encroachments were opposed—from Missouri to Kansas. The London *Times* has thus summed up the story for us :—

"Let there be no mistake as to *English* opinion on this subject. If we have paid a sincere homage to the rising greatness of America, it has not been to that which Southerners are anxious to preserve, but to that which they are striving to destroy. All that is noble and venerable in the United States is associated with its Constitution. It is not the demonstrations of Southern ruffianism in Congress; or the filibustering aggrandisement of the South; or the Fugitive Slave Law; or the Dred Scott decisions; or the Kansas-Nebraska Act;—it is not these, or any other, triumphs of Democratic insolence that have challenged the admiration of Europe. Mr. Lincoln will carry with him the support of those who, however tolerant of slavery, will not tamely acquiesce in its becoming the basis of an illegal and hostile confederacy."—Nov. 29, 1860.

And again :—

"No stretch of fanaticism on the part of the North has been so extravagant as the doctrines openly avowed by the South. In their passionate effrontery they have loudly declared that slavery, so far from being a blemish, is a positive blessing to a country; that it is the only true basis of labour, and the best cement of social institutions. They have claimed the right, not only of preserving it for the present, but of perpetuating it for all time, and of extending it into every territory annexed to the American Union. One by one they have set aside all barriers in the shape of limits and compromises, and have driven their principles, by sheer force, down the throats of their opponents."—Jan. 4, 1861.

"Eheu! fugaces, fugaces, anni!" The *Times, the* journal of all England, is now the avowed advocate of this very "illegal and hostile confederacy," and the champion of slavery out of the Bible.

But the North was thoroughly aroused by this accumulation of aggressions, and by the fact that her own trusted public men had contributed to her degradation. The Republican party almost triumphed in 1856, and was completely successful in 1860. Mr. Douglas, who had betrayed the interests of freedom and humanity, by consenting to the rupture of the Missouri Compromise, to gain Southern support in his Presidential canvass, was defeated, and Mr. Lincoln, pledged to the non-extension of slavery, was elected President of the United States.

But the ambition of the Pro-slavery party was not limited to the territory of the United States. Acting upon the conviction expressed by the Rev. Dr. Palmer, of New Orleans, that its "mission is to preserve and transmit to posterity its system of slavery, by obtaining for it the right to go and take root wherever nature and Providence can support it," the South has cast longing looks on neighbouring countries.

From 1849 to 1858, various attempts were made to invade and possess Cuba, by armed expeditions from the Southern coast, in secret understanding with malcontents on the island. But all these efforts failed, sometimes by the interference of the American Government, sometimes by the action of the Spanish authorities.

In furtherance of the same design, a Conference was held at Ostend, in 1854, between three of the United States' ministers accredited to foreign Courts. These men—Mr. Buchannan, of Pennsylvania, Mr. Mason, of Virginia, and Mr. Soulé, of Louisiana—prepared a manifesto,[1] which was made public. In this they had the monstrous effrontery to declare, "It is perfectly clear to every reflecting man that, by its geographical position, Cuba naturally belongs to the United States. . . . If Spain, deaf to the voice of her own interest, and impelled by blind pride and a false sentiment of honour, refuses to sell the island of Cuba to the United 'States, then, by all laws, human and divine, we shall have the right to snatch it from her if we are sufficiently powerful to do so." The Convention of the Democratic party, assembled at Cincinnati in 1856, substantially ratified this Ostend manifesto by choosing Mr. Buchannan, one of its authors, as the candidate of that party for the Presidency.

In 1858, Mr. Buchannan, elected President, proposed to Congress to carry out the Ostend programme. Mr. Slidell, now Confederate Commissioner to France, endeavoured to induce the Senate to allow the President a credit of $30,000,000 for the purpose of opening negotiations for the purchase of Cuba. And, at the same time, Mr. Mason, lately Confederate Commissioner to England, proposed that discretionary powers, including the employment of the naval and land forces of the United States, should be conferred upon the President, to facilitate this coveted acquisition. The Senate rejected both these propositions; but they clearly show the extreme lengths to which the South was willing to go, under the impulsion of two of the men who are now the most active agents of Southern independence, to secure the extension of slavery. Is it supposable that the Southern leaders

[1] "Les Etats-Unis en 1863," p. 130.

will be less determined, or less scrupulous, on behalf of their favourite institution, if the clog of Northern opposition shall be removed?

In 1854 occurred the marauding expedition of Walker against Nicaragua. His object was not only to re-establish slavery in that country, where it had been abolished, but also and especially to gain possession of a suitable base of operations against Cuba. His first purpose was temporarily accomplished: slavery was re-established by a Constitution prepared at New Orleans. But Walker and his party were soon driven out of the country.[1]

In view of the immense area of the Slave States, one is compelled to ask, What need had they of more territory? With a superficies of 550,000,000 of acres, of which not one-seventh part is cultivated, why should Southern slaveholders have coveted more? The answer is easy. *First,* they wanted new States "to redress the balance of the old." *Secondly,* they needed a boundless area of virgin soil to take the place of the lands exhausted by slave agriculture, which is so superficial, so careless, so expensive, and so limited in its range, as to render recuperation by rest, by rotation of crops, by manures, &c., impossible. Hence the vast majority of planters are obliged to forsake those lands from which they have reaped the first exuberance, and to take up fresh soil, which they abandon in turn after short cultivation. Judge Warner, in advocating, before the Legislature of Georgia, the necessity of continually extending Southern territory, gave the following reasons[2] for that necessity:—

"In this House, or out of it, who but knows perfectly well that, whenever slavery is confined within certain specified limits, its future existence is doomed? It is then only a question of time as to its final destruction. You may take any single slave-holding county in the Southern States, in which the great staples of cotton and sugar are cultivated to any extent, and confine the present slave population within the limits of that county. Such is the rapid natural increase of the slaves, and the rapid exhaustion of the soil in the cultivation of those crops (which add so much to the commercial wealth of the country), that in a few years it would be impossible to support them within the limits of such county. *Both master and slave would be starved out;* and what would be the practical effect in

---

[1] For a sketch of these various efforts of the South, see "Les Etats-Unis en 1863;" Ludlow's "History of the United States," &c. &c.

[2] *Daily News,* June 18th, 1863; see also Professor Cairnes' Remarks on Slave Agriculture, *op. cit.*

any one county, the same would happen in all the slaveholding States. Slavery cannot be confined within certain limits without producing the destruction of both master and slave; *it requires fresh lands*."

We shall have occasion to quote abundance of Southern testimony to prove that this exhausting effect of slave labour has taken place all over the Slave States.

By the election of Mr. Lincoln, the South saw that it was the evident determination of the Northern people that there should be no more acquisition of territory for slave culture, and that the old territory should not be prostituted to this purpose. Consequently, three courses lay before the Southern leaders: they must either submit to the starvation necessity, so logically predicted by Judge Warner; or they must themselves inaugurate a gradual Abolition policy; or they must secede from the Union, *for the express purpose, and with the calm determination, to acquire new territory, and a Government of their own.* They chose this last alternative,[1] and began the war by attacking Fort Sumter, and seizing upon United States' custom-houses, arsenals, post-offices, &c. &c.

But out of the Union, as in it, the same stern necessity for extension must urge the South to new conquests for continued existence, and each acquisition will but make the final destruction of the system, and the ruin of its abettors, more sure and

[1] The acquisition of the public territories has been for many years the grand object of Southern covetousness. In 1852, it assumed the form of a demand that Congress should not interfere at all with the matter, but should leave the settlers of those territories (from which it had been for ever excluded by the terms of the Missouri Compromise of 1820) to establish slavery therein, or to exclude it, as they might see fit. This was refused by the Democratic party of the North at that time, but was subsequently accepted by it in 1856, and, as the result, Mr. Buchannan was elected. In 1860, the South, not contented with this disposition of the question, which had been summarily rejected by the people of Kansas, where it was first tried, demanded that slavery should be *established by law* in all the territories. The Democratic party of the North, led by Mr. Douglas, did not dare to commit such a political suicide as this, and consequently Mr. Lincoln was elected President, simply in consequence of the split thus occasioned in the ranks of his opponents. (Letter published in the *Raleigh Standard*, of North Carolina, August, 1863; *Annuaire des Deux Mondes*, 1860; "Les Etats-Unis en 1863," &c. &c.) And even after the election of Mr. Lincoln, a delegation from the Border States waited upon him to endeavour to induce him to yield this point, in the hope of preventing war. The delegation insisted upon the right to carry slaves into the territories, and Mr. Lincoln refused. (Speech of Ex-Governor Moorhead, of Kentucky, delivered in England, quoted by Professor Cairnes in a Lecture on the American War.)

more disastrous. There is something transcendently impressive in the comprehensiveness and certainty of this retributive justice, by which slavery is made to avenge itself, by reason of the very evils which spring from it. Everywhere, those who have participated in the guilt are being made sharers in the punishment. Southern authorities, at all periods, have painted in darkest colours the deplorable effects of the institution upon Southern society—the poverty, the ignorance, the gross corruption of morals, the lawlessness, and crime.[1] The worst passions and propensities of the dominant race—ambition, pride, lust, cupidity, indolence—developed to their highest pitch, have returned to plague it for the injustice and cruelty it has wreaked upon the negro. The system might easily have been abolished, as was urged by the best and wisest, when the colonies themselves became free; it might have been abolished at any time since, with the glad assent of the North, had the South so willed it.[2] But, instead of abolition, we have had continual extension. And now, at last, to prevent for ever that consummation, the leaders of the South have inaugurated a civil war, without which, humanly speaking, abolition would have been impossible, but of which every day's continuance makes this result more sure. The whites have sent their fathers, husbands, sons, and brothers to fight for the preservation of slavery; scarce a house or a hut in

[1] In 1837, the Governor of Kentucky, in his message to the Legislature, said, "We long to see the day when the law shall assert its majesty, and stop the wanton destruction of life which almost daily occurs within the jurisdiction of this commonwealth. Men slaughter each other with almost perfect impunity," &c., &c. In the same year, the Governor of Alabama declared to the Legislature, "We hear of homicides in different parts of the State continually, and yet have few convictions, and still fewer executions. Why do we hear of *stabbings* and *shootings* almost daily in some part or other of our State?" The *New Orleans Bee*, of May 23, 1838, speaks of "this frightful deluge of human blood that flows through our streets and our places of public resort." (Mr. Sumner's "Speech on the Barbarism of Slavery," pp. 43, 44.)

[2] In 1826, a proposition was made in Congress that the proceeds of the sale of the public lands should be set apart, after the payment of the public debt, for the manumission of the slaves. In 1827, it was proposed that a national tax should be levied for the purchase and enfranchisement of all the slaves, at the average price of $250. At that time there was not quite a million of slaves in the country. Neither of these propositions was accepted by the South. At no time would the South accede to the proposition, often made, to purchase and free the slaves in the district of Columbia, the seat of the National Government. This was one of the first acts of Congress after the election of Mr. Lincoln.

all the land wherein is not one dead; but the slave, as the incarnation of so much gold, is shielded from danger and harm by the considerate selfishness of his master. Suffering and want seem to be the common lot of all the ruling race; yet from all these the slave is, as much as possible, shielded, that he may continue to be a slave.

> "But there's a Divinity that shapes our ends,
> Rough-hew them as we will."

Plagues, ten-fold worse than those which the immediate hand of God hurled upon the land of Egypt, have been brought upon the South by the deliberate acts of her own sons, that a bondage tenfold worse than that of Egypt shall be broken, and that an enslaved people shall become FREE.

But the South has no thought of submitting to this abandonment of slavery. All the prominent organs of the Southern press proclaim the opposite. Even the Financial Agent of the Confederacy in England, who may be supposed to have been informed of the sources whence his Government hopes to draw the wealth to enable it to pay its war-debt, and its future expenses, pictures in rapturous language its "empire in the future, extending from the home of Washington to the ancient palaces of Montezuma, uniting the proud old colonies of England with Spain's richest and most romantic dominions; combining the productions of the great valley of the Mississippi with the mineral riches, the magical beauty, the volcanic grandeur of Mexico—and commanding the materials of commerce throughout this wide expanse, from the Atlantic to the Pacific, no longer trammelled by the restrictions, nor taxed by the cupidity, of others."

How naturally this rich prospect makes the imagination of the financier to glow!

> "Ah non sapete
> I simpatici effetti prodigiosi,
> Che produce in lui la dolce idea dell' oro!
> All' idea di quel metallo
> Portentoso, onnipossente,
> Un vulcano la sua mente
> Già comincia a diventar."—*Figaro.*

But, presently, the Financial Agent, as if afraid of having allowed a weighty secret to escape him, of having exhibited too much of the fangs and terrible claws of his pet, reclothes it in the sheep-skin in which it suits the policy of the English friends of the South that the Confederacy should at present appear; and, a few pages further on says, "Be our ignorance of the merits of this question never so great, we behold a country of vast extent and large numbers earnestly desiring self-government. It threatens none, demands nothing, attacks no one, but wishes to rule itself and be let alone."[1]

[1] Spence's "American Union," pp. 287, 291.

IV.

THE RE-OPENING OF THE SLAVE-TRADE.

If fresh soil, without limit, be necessary to the existence of slavery, and to the continued prosperity of the South, *fresh slaves* is a far more pressing necessity. The former will be a want for future consideration; the latter is the great need of the day.

Hitherto, but $1\frac{634}{1000}$ per cent. of the land in the Slave States has been brought into cultivation. Its largest production of cotton in any one year was 5,196,944 bales, in 1860; while its capacity is estimated by Mr. De Bow at from 50 to 100 millions of bales annually, if the soil adapted to its culture could be worked. The demand for cotton has been continually increasing, at the average annual rate of 87,880 bales, of 450 pounds each, for the last ten years, from England alone; leaving a considerable deficiency to be supplied by inferior cotton from other countries than the Southern United States: which deficiency amounted, in 1860, to more than 386,000 bales for England. Besides the English demand, there is considerably more than one-half as much to be furnished to other manufacturing nations. The price has risen steadily, notwithstanding the steady augmentation in the supply. In 1844-5, the crop was 2,394,503 bales, of 400 pounds each, and the average price was $8\frac{3}{4}$ cents per pound, in Liverpool. In 1859-60, the crop was 4,675,770 bales, and the price 11 cents per pound. Everything, in short, has been favourable—soil, climate, demand, increasing price—to the production of as much American cotton as would be required to supply all demands at a fair remuneration, excepting one requisite only, namely, *an abundance of labour*. And here we have the astounding obstacle, that the higher the price of cotton, the less remunerative, under slave labour, does the cultivation of cotton become. Mr. De Bow declares that "the great limitation to the production of cotton is the scarcity of labour. *Whenever cotton rises to ten cents per pound, labour becomes too dear to increase production rapidly*"—*i.e.* under the stimulus of high prices for cotton, the demand for slaves occasions such an advance in their value, that cotton-planting almost ceases to be profitable. It is estimated[1] that *each additional cent* per pound in the price of cotton, *adds one hundred dollars to the average cost of slaves* in the United States.

How is this difficulty to be obviated? is the problem which has long perplexed the Southern mind. *Free labour* had already begun to assist in its solution: even in 1850, under the spur of high prices, one-ninth of all the cotton produced was by free labour, and the amount has gone on increasing. But free white labourers are tabooed in slave countries; the native whites, for the most part, consider field-labour as degrading, and slavery prevents the immigration of whites who would be willing to work. Hence, the cotton-crop must be almost entirely dependant upon slave labour, so long as slavery endures as the predominant system.

The internal slave-trade has failed to supply the amount of labour requisite to the demands of the cotton-growing States, although it is computed[2] that, from 1840 to 1860, no less than 488,258 slaves, most of them able-bodied labourers, had been sold from the Northern Slave States, at a cost of about *two hundred millions of dollars.*

The African slave-marts alone could satisfy the craving demands of the Cotton States. Consequently, it has been towards a re-opening of the African slave-trade that Southern policy has been directed. But under the Union, and especially

[1] Stirling's "Letters from the Slave States," p. 305.

[2] "Report of the Boston Board of Trade to the Government, for 1863." We are happy to acknowledge our indebtedness to that valuable publication for the facts we have given above. The author says that the increase of the slave population of the United States, from 1840 to 1850, was in the ratio of 28·91 per cent., which, applied to the eight principal cotton States, would give an increase of 240,313 slaves. The actual increase, however, was 537,939, showing an importation from the Northern Slave States of 297,626 during that decade. The ratio of increase from 1850 to 1860 was 23·35 per cent., which would have given for the cotton States an increase of 422,464 slaves; the actual increase was 613,096, showing an importation of 190,632 during that period (p. 109).

under the supremacy of Northern principles, such as were clearly indicated in the election of Mr. Lincoln, the re-opening of the African slave-trade was an impossibility. Hence the leaders of the South determined to throw off this obstacle. Secession, therefore, was undertaken in order to fulfil the two-fold necessity of Southern policy—*indefinite supply of land, and free-trade in slaves.*

For more than ten years this latter topic has occupied the attention of Southern economists. Among the first movers in the matter was Mr. Yancey, Senator from Alabama. He did not hesitate to proclaim that free-trade in negroes was just as legitimate a branch of commerce "as free-trade in donkeys or nutmegs," and that it was vastly more essential to the prosperity of the South than free-trade in any other sort of merchandise. Mr. Yancey, it will be remembered, was the first Commissioner chosen by the Confederate Government to represent it at the Court of Abolition England. In fact, the very men who have all along been the most active in the development of this cardinal feature of Southern policy are they who are foremost in the Government of the Confederacy, and in furthering its plans abroad.

The idea of free-trade in negroes rapidly became popularized, the more so, as it opened the way by which the possession of slaves might become much more general amongst the whites than it has been, or ever could be, under the monopoly of the Border States. Soon it became a prominent subject of discussion at public meetings. In 1856, at a Commercial Convention held in Savannah, the re-opening of the African slave-trade was publicly debated; even the delegates from Virginia advocated the measure.[1] The Hon. L. W. Spratt, of South Carolina, said, "The first reason for its revival is, that it will give political power to the South. Imported slaves will increase our representation in the National Legislature. More slaves will give us more States; and it is, therefore, within the power of the rude, untutored savages we may bring from Africa, to restore to the South the influence she has lost by the suppression of the trade. *We want only that kind of population which will extend and secure our peculiar institutions*, and there is no other source but Africa." Mr. Stephens, now Vice-President of the Southern

[1] Ludlow's "History of the United States," p. 264.

Confederacy, declared, "We can divide Texas into five Slave States, *and get Chihuaha, Sonora*, &c., if we have the slave population; and it is plain that, unless the number of the African stock be increased, we have not the population, and we might as well abandon the race with our Northern brethren in the colonization of the territories. Slave States cannot be made without Africans. I am not telling you to do it; but it is a serious question concerning our political and domestic policy; and it is useless to wage war about abstract rights, or to quarrel and accuse each other of unsoundness, unless we get more Africans. *Negro slavery is but in its infancy.*" And Mr. Jefferson Davis, now the President of the Confederacy, while objecting to the re-opening of the foreign slave-trade, so far as the interests of Mississippi were concerned, earnestly disclaimed "any coincidence of opinion with those *who prate of the inhumanity and sinfulness of the trade.* The interest of Mississippi, not of the African," said he, "dictates my conclusion. Her arm is, no doubt, strengthened by a due proportion of the servile caste, but it might be paralyzed by such an afflux as would probably follow if the gates of the African slave-market were thrown open. This conclusion, in relation to Mississippi, is based upon my view of her present condition, not upon general theory. It is not supposed to be applicable to Texas, to New Mexico, or *to any future acquisitions to be made south of the Rio Grande.*"[1]

In 1857, the Governor of South Carolina, in his annual message to the Legislature, denounced the constitutional prohibition of the trade, "as it discriminated in opposition to the interests of the South." And Southern Congressmen[2] at Washington did not hesitate to inveigh against the law on this subject.

The Southern press advocated the restoration. The *Charleston Standard* proposed, "as a leading principle of the Southern policy, to re-open and legitimate the slave-trade." The *True Southern*, of Mississippi, suggested "the propriety of stimulating the zeal of the pulpit by founding a prize for the best sermon in favour of free-trade in negroes."

At a popular Convention held at Vicksburgh in May, 1859,

[1] Cairnes, "The Slave Power," pp. 242, 243.

[2] Ibid. p. 240.

a vote in favour of the trade was passed by a large majority; and this was followed up by the formation of an "African Labour-Supply Association," of which Mr. De Bow, the editor of the leading Southern review, was elected president. In Alabama, a "League of United Southerners" pronounced the prohibition of the foreign slave-trade to have been an unworthy concession to the demands of Northern fanaticism, and insisted on "the necessity of sustaining slavery, not only where its existence is put directly in issue, but where it is remotely concerned." In the Legislatures of Louisiana and Arkansas Bills advocating it were passed in the Lower Houses, and lost in the Senates of those States only by a small majority. In Georgia, the Executive Committee of an Agricultural Society offered "a premium of twenty-five dollars for the best specimen of a live African, imported within the last twelve months, to be exhibited at the next meeting of the Society." And in fact, many slavers did unquestionably land their cargoes upon the Southern coast in 1859-60.[1] Thus the scheme was fairly launched, even before secession, and while the United States law condemned the slave-trade as piracy, and punished the convicted trader with death.

In 1857-58 the Government was made to aid in the accomplishment of the Southern policy, by protesting against the restricted visitation of suspected slavers under the American flag, on the part of British cruisers. In consequence of the removal of this check, the slave-trade increased immensely. At the same time,[2] Mr. Slidell, the present Confederate Commissioner to France, urged the Senate to order the withdrawal of the United States' cruisers from the coast of Africa, thus removing the only remaining obstacle, imperfect as it had been, to the desecration of the American flag. But the Senate rejected the demand.

It may be objected that all the above facts occurred before secession, and that since that event the sentiment of the South is no longer favourable to the re-opening of the slave-trade with Africa. We shall see how utterly unfounded is this amiable supposition.

The first Congress of the Southern States, composed of dele-

[1] Cairnes, "The Slave Power."
[2] "Les Etats-Unis en 1863."

gates from the six States which at that time had seceded from the Union, met in February, 1861. Among its members were those who were engaged in forming, if they had not already drawn up, the Constitution of the new Confederacy. One of the first Acts of this Congress was a Bill to revive the African slave-trade, not avowedly (for this would have shocked many Southerners, and would have astonished and disgusted England, perhaps), but by so modifying the United States' law as really to encourage the traffic. This Confederate Bill proposed to consider the African slave-trade as a mere infraction of Southern law, and to punish the offender by *publicly selling the slaver and its cargo for the benefit of the State.* The South could desire nothing more than that such seizures and sales should take place very frequently: but no seizure would be likely to be made, for there would probably be no informer against any humane and enterprising Christian who had exposed himself and his property to considerable risk, to say nothing of the opprobrium, for the purpose of conferring so great a boon upon the cotton States. President Davis, of course, *vetoed* this Bill in a secret message to the Confederate Congress. The President's assigned reasons for his *veto* were based, undoubtedly, upon the necessities of the Confederacy as regards conciliating European sentiment. His own opinions, as we have seen, were by no means hostile to the object of the Bill, and his associates in the Government, and people of all classes, were in favour of the same, as we have shown. The mere passage of such a measure through the Confederate Congress, only a few days after its assembly, clearly shows that the re-opening of the slave-trade with Africa was the predominating desire of Southern legislators.[1]

It is true that, by the Confederate Constitution, "the importation of negroes of the African race, from any foreign country other than the slave-holding States or territories of the United States of America, is forbidden," and that "Congress is required to pass such laws as shall effectually prevent the same;" "shall also have power to prohibit the introduction of slaves from any State not a member of, or territory not belonging to, the Confederacy." But the purpose of these clauses is too apparent to need explanation: the first was intended to conciliate Europe, and especially England, while it offered a direct bribe to the

[1] *Annuaire des Deux Mondes,* 1861, pp. 585, 586.

Border Slave States which had not yet seceded, and which seemed indisposed to secede, from the Union. The last clause was tantamount to a declaration to those States: "If you don't join us we will not purchase your slaves, and then there can be no salvation possible for you." The amusing contradiction between these clauses of the Confederate Constitution and those others which directly provide for the maintenance and extension of slavery,[1] taken in connexion with the avowed policy of the leading men of the South for the preceding ten years, the Bill passed by the Confederate Congress to which we have just alluded, the acknowledged pressing need of additional slave-labour, and the declared object of the South in seceding,—this contradiction is, we say, too flagrant to excite anything but laughter at the idea that it could impose upon any one.

It is notorious that great and general dissatisfaction was expressed at these prohibitory clauses of the Constitution. Thus *The Southern Confederacy*, a journal of Florida, remarked upon them: "For God's sake, and for the sake of consistency, let us not form a Union *for the express purpose of maintaining and propagating African slavery*, and then, as the Southern Congress has just done, confess our error by enacting a constitutional provision abolishing the African slave-trade! The re-opening of this trade is a mere matter of expediency, to be determined by legislative enactment hereafter."[2]

But the strongest protest against these clauses of the Constitution was from the pen of Mr. Spratt, entitled "The Philosophy of Secession," from which we have already quoted. Mr. Spratt contends that the double object of the South should be "to preserve the rounded form of a social aristocracy" given originally by slavery, and to increase the number of its slaves. Neither of these, he says, can be accomplished unless the African slave-trade be re-opened. He argues that to the just constitution of a slave society as many slaves as whites are necessary. In all the Border Slave States the whites are daily getting more and more in excess of the blacks, in consequence of the drain of the latter to the cotton States, so that those States have become democratized, lukewarm in their attachment to slavery, and half-hearted in their allegiance to the Confederacy. He even

[1] *Ante*, p. 33.

[2] Cairnes, *op. cit.* p. 290.

fears that a similar democratizing process may take place in South Carolina, "the purest in its slave condition," for he finds that slaves are constantly being drawn away not only from the towns but also from the rural districts of that State, to supply the south-western demand; that the whites, of the poorer non-slave-holding sort, will grow more and more exacting in their claims for political power, and that South Carolina will be more ruined, if possible, than ever.

The need of the African slave-trade to furnish labourers for Southern fields is too obvious to need proof, in Mr. Spratt's judgment.

Mr. Spratt thinks very little of the objections urged against the scheme. As to any danger to be apprehended from slave insurrections, when the slaves are under "an ordinary state of martial law, as perfect as that which, in times of popular outbreak, is the last and surest provision for security and order," he thinks it amounts to nothing. The necessity of consulting foreign opinion and sentiment is not to be thought of. So long as France and England trade in coolies; so long as "England lends her ships to keep the slave-trade open in the Black Sea, and almost every slave bought in Africa is paid for in English fabrics, to the profit of the English merchant, and with the knowledge of the British Government, it were simple to suppose that European States will practise sentiment at the expense of interest. . . As they have no repugnance to slavery in accordance with their interests, so also can they have none to the extension of it. They will submit to any terms of intercourse with the slave republic in consideration of its markets and products. An increase of slaves will increase the market and supply. They will pocket their philanthropy and the profits together."[1]

There is, unfortunately, no doubt that Mr. Spratt took a more correct measure of the comparative importance of principle as against interest, on this question, in the estimation of the vast majority of the noble and cultivated classes of Englishmen, as well as of the commercial classes, than we of the North did, at the commencement of the war.

An intercepted despatch from the Confederate Secretary of State to its Commissioner at St. Petersburgh, throws some light

[1] Appendix to Prof. Cairnes, *op. cit.*

on the intentions of the Government of the Confederacy. The Commissioner is directed, in case an attempt should be made by the Russian Government to introduce into any treaty or negociation any stipulation binding the Confederacy not to re-open the slave-trade, to "assume the position that the consitution of the Confederacy is a compact entered into between independent States, in other words, that no power has been delegated to the Government on the subject," &c., &c.[1]

From all the preceding considerations we think the conclusion is unavoidable, that it is the deliberate intention of the Confederate Government, or of "the sovereign States" of the Confederacy, to re-open the slave-trade with Africa as soon as practicable. In fact, from the evidence we have adduced, it seems to us quite obvious that this measure is absolutely essential to the progress of the South under its present economic system.

Many intelligent people in England profess the belief that slavery is more likely to be abolished under Southern independence than if the United States' Government should succeed in reducing the rebellion. Some people are capable of believing anything, and the more improbable the story, the more thoroughly, if not always the more readily, it is often believed. The supernatural itself inspires a sort of credence. It was even said that Mr. Slidell had assured M. Emile de Girardin, in Paris, that "the South was disposed to disencumber itself of slavery, which was rather injurious than advantageous to it." This statement reached America, and Mr. Slidell was obliged to contradict it. In a letter from Paris to the *Courier des Etats-Unis*, of New York,[2] we read, "Mr. Slidell acknowledges that he said to M. Girardin that the slaves, once free, must leave the South, which would not tolerate a mingling of the two races, and that the expatriation of the negroes was at once the condition of their emancipation and the difficulty. *But he has not declared that the South was disposed to disencumber itself of slavery*, which was more injurious than advantageous to it. Mr. Slidell could not have made such a declaration for three reasons. The first is, that he has no authority to make it, and that the Govern-

[1] *Journal des Débats*, April 22, 1863.
[2] April 3, 1863.

ment would no more have it than he, as the question of emancipation can only be raised by the several States, and not by the Central Government. The second is, that if slavery is destined to disappear one day, or to be modified like all human institutions, *this would not take place on the morrow of a revolution, when the first necessity of the South will be to repair its losses.* The third reason is, that the South means to decide this question in full liberty, by its sole authority, and will not make it, in any event, the condition of its recognition by Europe."

About the same time, the *Richmond Examiner*, supposed to be the chief exponent of the Government in the press, declared, "The establishment of the Confederacy is a distinct reaction against the mistaken civilization of the age. For 'liberty, equality, fraternity,' we have deliberately substituted slavery, subordination, government. Reverently, we feel that our Confederacy is a God-sent missionary to the nations with great truths to preach. . . There are men in these Confederate States who have long deeply and earnestly striven to express, though timidly and speculatively, on what foundations of fact, with what corner-agents of principle, our social institution was one day to be built up fair and bright. Let them speak out in no apologetic tone, nor place us, at their peril, in any deprecautious attitude. This people has surely won the right 'to be let alone.' They will accept no deduction in politics, in literature, in philosophy; they will not follow, but lead; not borrow, but lend. They are more than content with their own principle of morals and way of life, and will stand upon it to the end, so help them God."[1]

From a careful consideration of all the facts contained in the foregoing pages, we can draw no other conclusion than that the South is thoroughly determined to sink or swim with slavery.

We do not wish to conceal or extenuate the disgraceful truth that the Slave States have been very materially aided in all their designs, previous to the election of Mr. Lincoln, by influential men and associations of the North. The Democratic party was always in alliance with the South, until that alliance was thrown up by the South itself at the Baltimore and Charleston Conventions, in 1860. In fact the leaders of the secession movement

[1] May 28, 1863; the article is quoted in full in the London *Daily News*, June 15, 1863.

counted largely for their success upon the secret or open aid of their old allies. Nor have they been altogether disappointed. Many, more or less prominent, leaders of the Democratic party at the North have manifested a strong desire and determination to aid them, by throwing all sorts of obstacles in the way of the Government. Under the mask of devotion to popular rights and individual liberty, as guaranteed by the Constitution, these men are the most dangerous enemies to both. They know that their own hold on political power is seriously endangered, if not lost, unless the Union be restored upon its original basis, and their former alliance with the Southern slaveholders renewed. They belong to that class which the immortal Florentine has so well described:

> " A quel cattivo coro
> Degli Angeli, che non furon ribelli,
> Nè fur fedeli a Dio, ma per se foro."

But the South had other allies at the North. The system of labour which, by confining the resources of the South to a single branch of industry, and chiefly to a single product of agriculture, rendered the Slave States tributary to the capitalists and manufacturers of the North, made these thereby immediately interested in the permanence of "the institution." One of the first results of secession was, to cancel by one act of confiscation or sequestration, the Southern debt to Northern creditors of $300,000,000. Again, the mass of the Northern people, even of the more intelligent, had no adequate conception of the true nature and results of slavery, in its various economic, political and moral phases, nor of the extreme lengths to which the Southern leaders would go; these people were accustomed to see slavery through Southern spectacles. Even earnest patriots, who really understood "this mystery of iniquity," and who saw the danger it was bringing upon the whole country, and its corrupting effects upon the entire nation, hesitated to oppose its continued encroachments with all the energy and promptitude the magnitude of the evil demanded, lest the very crisis we are now encountering should be brought about. And, worst of all, the most influential religious bodies of the North, which should have been the watchmen to sound the alarm, cried " peace and safety, when destruction was upon us ; " they feared to disturb the false tranquillity for which they themselves were, to a great degree, answerable,[1] lest the drowsy peace of the Church should be broken, and the funds for religious enterprises be lessened. It is but a just punishment, therefore, that the North should suffer for the crime, in the profits and guilt of which it has been so largely participant. Both North and South needed this terrible convulsion of all their social and political elements, in order that their moral atmosphere should become purified, and that the people should learn that, in God's government of the universe, national sins are visited by national punishments.

But, at last, the North, by a variety of considerations, some of which are noble, and others less so, has become awakened to a sense of its duty. Let its people persevere until that duty shall have been thoroughly and well accomplished. Let the Government persist in conquering the rebellion, until slavery, its cause and object, shall have perished with it. This it is bound to do, in order to vindicate in the eyes of its loyal subjects, and of foreign nations, its violated authority; by its duty to maintain over all its domain the common rights of all its citizens, purchased by their common resources and common sacrifices; by the trust committed to it "to establish justice, ensure domestic tranquillity, promote the general welfare, and secure the blessings of liberty to ourselves and our posterity;" by its sacred obligations to humanity, outraged in this monstrous attempt to legalize oppression. It is already a great step taken in the path of justice to have begun to abolish so great a wrong as slavery. Patriotism, intelligence, Christianity, will not be wanting to counteract and alleviate the evils which this abolition may occasion. Let us perform, with our whole hearts, to-day the duty which lies immediately before us, and let the morrow take thought for the things of itself.

We cannot leave this branch of our subject without acknowledging our debt of gratitude, and rendering our tribute of praise,

[1] That portion of the great Presbyterian body which, after the division of that sect, was known as the *Old School*, and to which the Southern presbyteries adhered, had always refused to take a decided stand against slavery. The other portion, the *New School*, was desirous that the Presbyterian Church should declare itself strongly against that institution. Since the war there has been a decided disposition manifested amongst the two parties at the North to re-unite. This looks very much as though slavery had been the *teterrima causa* of their quarrel, rather than mere doctrinal differences.

to those few men—Garrison, and Gerrit Smith, and Sumner, and Howe, and others—the early apostles of abolition, of whom the country was not worthy. We honour them now as we disliked them once, as being "pestilent fellows," and men of one idea. But all men who inaugurate great reformations must be pestilent fellows to the men of their day, until their work has been accomplished; then their worth is recognised; "their works do follow them." Such men must be men of one idea. This single purpose they must carry about with them at all times; they must incessantly kindle it afresh from their own glowing souls into new life, or it will die in the uncongenial atmosphere in which they move. Thus it was with Howard, and with Wilberforce, and Father Matthew; thus it was, and still is, with our own Miss Dix, who, wherever she goes—and where has she not journeyed, over America, and Europe, and the far East?—carries with her the one idea of mercy to the prisoner, the sick, and the insane; thus it was with John Knox, and Calvin, and Luther; thus it was with Peter the Hermit; thus it was with St. Paul, with his "*this one thing I do.*" People always call such men *fanatics;* they must be fanatics, or they will accomplish nothing in the face of the opposition which besets them. And so the early Abolitionists of the United States were fanatics, but they are the Regenerators of America, the Fathers of the second American Independence. Let their zeal, and their intelligence, and their unselfish patriotism live and work among us, until the great work which they began shall be thoroughly done—until every American shall be free.

V.

THE EFFECTS OF SLAVERY UPON THE SOCIAL CONDITION OF THE SOUTHERN PEOPLE.

THE settlement of the Northern and Southern Colonies was made at about the same time, so that the differences in their social progress, which we are about to exhibit, can in no wise be attributed to difference in age. Virginia, the first of the Southern Colonies, was established in 1607; New York, the earliest of the Northern, was settled in 1614. But there was a marked difference between the first colonists: those of the Northern section, particularly of New England, were industrious, respectable people, rarely connected with noble European families. They left their native land in search of civil and religious liberty. Generally belonging to the reformed religion, as religious reformists of every name have always done when they have had the power, they denied to non-conformists the liberty which they prized so much for themselves. But they were rigid in their ideas of public and private virtue, they did not tolerate immorality, and they honoured labour and industry. On the other hand, the settlers of the Southern Colonies were, many of them, members of more or less noble English families, whose personal fortunes were ruined by extravagance and vice; others were criminals, political or religious offenders, or adventurers who had escaped from justice, or had been transported as punishment, or had been sold by the favourites of the court as slaves to work in the colonies, or who had gone thither in search of fortune. All these were miserable elements in a society which could not prosper, save by the industry, zeal, and good conduct of its individual members. The few really good colonists were speedily contaminated by the bad example of the majority. The early history of the Colony of Virginia, as told by Smith and Beverley, is a tale of indolence, lawlessness, immorality and failure. The reputation of the colony, even in the London prisons, which contributed to it so many of their inmates, was such that Smith wrote, "Some did choose to be hanged ere they would go thither, *and were*." This condition of things was necessarily made worse by the importation, in 1620 and subsequently, of negroes from Africa, who, by their colour, savage habits, and low type of humanity, tended to make labour, in the estimation of the white population, more and more degrading.

The colonists of the Carolinas were not essentially different from those of Virginia, and their histories are not dissimilar in any important respect. Georgia was at first settled exclusively by honest, industrious and well-behaved poor people from the British towns and, subsequently, from the rural population. Slavery was expressly prohibited by the colonial charter; but after some years, the colonists were tempted by the vicinity of the slave-holding Carolinas to insist that slavery should be established amongst themselves also. After long and violent discussions between one party which favoured, and another which opposed it, the boon was granted by the king, who resumed the proprietorship of the colony.[1]

Let us first examine into the effects of Slavery upon the EDUCATIONAL progress of the Southern States.

One of the advantages claimed for slavery is, that it enables the dominant class to devote itself to intellectual pursuits, to cultivate the arts and graces of social life, and to acquire a knowledge of the political administration of the country.[2] We submit, on the contrary, that in all these respects, slavery has been a hindrance, and that in others of equal, or greater moment, it has been positively fatal to progress. It is the North which has established the prosperity and good reputation of the United States. Almost every American name known to Europe in literature, in science, in art, belongs to the North. Almost all the great and useful enterprises of the country, its com-

[1] See the various histories of the United States, and the early English Colonies of America; Colton's "Progress of the United States;" Olmsted's "Seaboard Slave States," &c. &c.

[2] Address of Governor Hammond, of South Carolina, in the *Southern Literary Messenger*.

mercial and industrial successes, are due to Northern capital, energy, and intelligence. It is the North which has established all the great religious and educational institutions of the land. And the reason of this is obvious. By degrading labour, slavery has paralysed the mass of the white population of the South; by accumulating the wealth, the education, and the honours of the country in the hands of a very few persons, it has necessarily limited the number and lessened the force of the ordinary stimuli to exertion, even to these few; by vitiating the general standard of excellence, it has contracted the capacities and lowered the aims even of the best. In political life, one can perceive the advantage of possessing a class of intelligent and liberal men who have made political science a study, and who may carry out from generation to generation any given line of policy, *if that policy be good;* but slavery has created for the South a policy, the exigences of which have at length brought ruin upon itself, and vast misery upon the whole land.

From the earliest period, education has been neglected at the South. The sons of some of the more wealthy planters were sent to England for instruction, but the number who received this advantage was very small. So lightly esteemed was education, as a popular privilege, that Sir William Berkeley, the Governor of Virginia in 1640, said, "Thank God, there are no free-schools nor printing-offices here, and I hope we shall not have any for an hundred years." In the New England colonies, on the other hand, popular education was one of the first objects of legislation. Only eighteen years after Massachusetts was founded, Harvard University was established. There were five printing-offices and as many book-stores in the town of Boston alone, at a period when there was not one of either in Virginia and the Carolinas.[1]

It has been more and more felt in the Free States that, in a country which was yearly receiving such an influx of foreigners in addition to the increase of its native population, and in which the franchise is almost unrestricted, the only salvation for its free institutions is to provide proper religious and intellectual training for all. And nobly has this conviction been acted upon, in all the Free States of the Union.

Mr. Howison, the historian of Virginia, describes the upper classes of that colony, about the middle of the last century, as

[1] Olmsted, *op. cit.*; Ludlow's "History of the United States."

" an aristocracy neither of talent, nor of learning, nor of moral worth, but of landed and slave interest." And of the people in his own day (1848) he says, " The question might be asked, Where is the literature of Virginia? and it would not be easily answered. It is a melancholy fact, that her people have never been a reading people. In the mass they have shown an indifference to polite literature and education in general, which is depressing to the mind that wishes to see them respectable and happy. It is with pain that we are compelled to speak of *the horrible cloud of ignorance* that rests on Virginia." He estimates that of the 166,000 white youths in the State, between the ages of seven and sixteen, 126,000 attended no school at all, and received no education whatever. Besides these, he counts 449,087 slaves, and 48,852 free blacks, with few exceptions, wholly uneducated. He continues, " *The policy which discourages further extension of knowledge among them is necessary*; but the fact remains unchanged that they exist among us,—a huge mass of mind almost entirely unenlightened. We fear that the most favourable estimate will leave in our State 683,000 *rational beings who are destitute of the merest rudiments of knowledge.*"[1] The total population of Virginia in 1848, was about 1,400,000.

The more intelligent portion of the planters do not neglect the education of their own children; these are taught at home, or in Southern seminaries, or, more commonly, perhaps, in Northern institutions. But for the education of the *people*, scarce anything has been done by the class which possesses all the wealth, and makes the laws of the Slave States. It is urged with truth that there " a perfect system of common school education is almost an impossibility;" that " extensive plantations, occupied by slaves only, independently of the exhausting crops they produce and by which the number of barren fields is continually increased, render a system of common schools impossible," by reason of the sparseness and poverty of the population.[2] But not only this, the vast majority of the white population seems to have little or no desire for intellectual improvement. Hence Mr. Gregg, in an address before the South Carolina Institute, said, " While we are aware that the Northern and Eastern States of the Union find

1 Olmsted, *op. cit.* pp. 172, 173.

2 "An Historical Sketch of Slavery," by Mr. Cobb, of Georgia, quoted by Ludlow, *op. cit.* p. 189.

no difficulty in educating their poor, we ourselves are ready to despair of success in this matter. Even penal laws against the neglect of education would fail to induce our country-people to send their children to school."[1]

And yet the advocates of slavery are constantly striving to extend the system more and more, which will still farther contribute to the poverty and sparseness of the population, and render any system of common education still more impossible.

The governors of several of the Slave States have repeatedly urged the legislatures to endeavour to remedy this difficulty. Governor Seabrook, of South Carolina, in 1848, reminded the Legislature that " Education had been provided by the State but for one class of citizens,—the wealthy class. For the middle and poorer classes of society it has done nothing, since no organized system has been adopted for that purpose. . . . Ten years ago, 20,000 adults (considerably more than one-fourth of the entire adult white population of the State), besides children, were unable to read or write, in South Carolina." And he asks, " Has our free-school system dispelled any of this ignorance? Are there no reasonable fears that the number has increased since?" In 1855, Governor Adams, of the same State, urged the Legislature to " make at least this effort, and if it results in nothing,—if, in consequence of insurmountable difficulties in our condition, no improvement can be made on the present system, *and the poor of the land are hopelessly doomed to ignorance, poverty, and crime,*—you will, at least, feel conscious of having done your duty, and the public anxiety on the subject will be quieted."[2]

In 1837, the Governor of Kentucky announced that one-third of its adult white population were unable to write their names. The Governor of Virginia declared, the same year, that of 4,614 applicants for marriage licences, no less than 1,047 were unable to sign their names.[3] The superintendent of public schools in Louisiana recently recommended to the Legislature to insist that " at least two out of three of the *Directors of common schools* should be able to read and write;"[4] and he declared that in one of the parishes into which the State is divided, twelve different directors had affixed their marks instead of their signatures to the certificates of school-teachers.

1 Cairnes, *op. cit.* p. 153.
2 Helper, *op. cit.* p. 434.
3 Olmsted, *op. cit.* p. 505.
4 Ludlow, *op. cit.* p. 190.

A Southerner who had resided in Mexico, and had lived many years in South Carolina, in speaking to Mr. Olmsted of the population of extensive communities on the banks of the Congaree, in that State, said, "They are more ignorant, their superstitions are more degrading, they are much less patient and industrious, far less cheerful and happy, and very much more incapable of being improved and elevated, than the most degraded *pœons* of Mexico."[1]

Mr. Lumpkin, of Georgia, speaks of "our poor, degraded, half-fed, half-clothed, and ignorant population—without Sabbath-schools, or any other means of instruction, mental or moral, and without any just appreciation of character."[2]

Mr. Olmsted says of the white inhabitants of the vast pine-forest districts of North Carolina, that "the negroes are decidedly superior to the great mass of them in every intellectual and moral respect."[3]

So much for the education of the white population of the Slave States.

The law in most or all of these States expressly prohibits the education of the *Blacks,* whether slave or free, on the alleged ground of the danger which would result to the public safety. And the friends of slavery urge that to educate the slaves would only make them more discontented with their lot and more unhappy. But, it may well be asked, who gave the right to hold the mind as well as the body of the negro in slavery, and to prevent the development of whatever faculties his Maker imparted to him? And, moreover, if one of the advantages of slavery to the negro be, as it is pretended, to elevate and christianise him, do not the very slave-laws prevent such results?

At the North, the number of black youths and children at the public schools is greater in proportion than that of the whites so educated at the South. In Massachusetts, one-sixth of the black population, between five and twenty years of age, is instructed at the public expense, and in the same schools with the whites.[4]

According to the census of 1850, the population of the Free States was composed of 13,268,470 whites, and 196,116 blacks;

[1] Olmsted, *op. cit.* pp. 505, 506.

[2] Helper, *op. cit.* p. 405.

[3] Helper, *op. cit.* pp. 348, 349.

[4] Ludlow, *op. cit.* p. 191.

that of the Slave States 6,184,477 whites, 228,128 free negroes, and 3,200,304 slaves.

In the Slave States, 8·37 per cent. of the adult native whites, and 9·09 per cent. of the adult foreign whites, were unable to read or write. In the Free States the proportions were 2·40 per cent. of the former, and 6·37 per cent. of the latter. In Virginia the proportion of the ignorant population was 20 per cent.; in North Carolina, 25 per cent.

In the Free States, the number of public schools was 62,433, or one for every 215 of the entire population; in the Slave States, 18,507, or one for every 519 of the aggregate population. The number of pupils in the Free States educated at the public expense, was 2,769,901, at a cost of $6,760,335. In the Slave States there were 581,801 pupils, and the expense of instruction was $2,719,530. Besides the system of public schools, both sections of the country have their respective seminaries, colleges, universities, &c., with regard to which the same superiority in every respect pertains to the Free States, as in the case of the public schools.[1]

Sabbath-schools are probably more numerous and more numerously attended in the United States than in any other country, and constitute a very important feature of the public instruction of the country. In the Free States alone, there were more than 3,000,000 Sunday-school pupils, instructed by more than 400,000 male and female teachers. The whole system is supported by voluntary contribution, the States being in no way connected with it.

Another important element in the public educational means

[1] Since 1790, Congress has granted aid to all the States for educational purposes to an immense extent: for *Public Schools,* 1,280 acres of public lands in every township of 23,040 acres (80,555,555 acres), being worth at the minimum price $100,694,443, but the real value in money received being much greater: for *Colleges* and *Universities,* 12,080,000 acres (including 3,553,824 acres granted to the State of Tennessee), worth, at the minimum Government price, $15,100,000. In 1836, after full payment of the entire principal and interest of the Public Debt, there remained in the Treasury of the United States a surplus of $38,000,000, of which about one-half was divided amongst the States for educational purposes. These Congressional grants are exclusive of the many millions expended upon the National Naval and Military Schools. Besides these public donations, the individual States of the Union, territories, counties, cities, and towns have granted in aid of education, it is estimated, no less than an additional $148,000,000, within their respective jurisdictions, since 1790—making in all $282,794,443. (Mr. Walker's fifth "Letter on American Finances and Resources," pp. 10, 11.)

provided in the Free States, consists in the various institutions at which free courses of public lectures are given on numerous branches of art and science; scarce a large town in any of the Free States which has not some such organization, endowed or supported by voluntary contributions. These lectures are usually given at night, so that they may be frequented by the industrious mechanic and artisan who is desirous of improving himself.

In 1860, the number of journals, periodicals, &c. &c., published in the Free States was 3,172, with a circulation of 760,034,360 annually; in the Slave States, 879 publications, with an annual circulation of 167,917,188 copies.[1]

In 1850, in the former States, there were 14,911 public libraries, containing 3,888,234 volumes; in the latter, 695 libraries, with an aggregate of 649,577 volumes.

Of patents for useful and ingenious inventions, 4,059 were issued to citizens of the North, and 625 to those of the South.

Mr. Goodrich, in his "Recollections of a Lifetime," thus sums up the value of the books published and sold in the United States, from 1820 to 1850, inclusive:—

Designation.	1820.	1830.	1840.	1850.
Elementary books	$750,000	$1,000,000	$2,000,000	$5,000,000
Classical	250,000	350,000	550,000	1,000,000
Theological	150,000	250,000	300,000	500,000
Legal	200,000	300,000	400,000	700,000
Medical	150,000	200,000	250,000	400,000
Miscellaneous	1,000,000	1,300,000	2,000,000	4,400,000
Total	$2,500,000	$3,400,000	$5,500,000	$12,000,000

In 1860, the value of the books, journals, &c., published in the United States was $39,678,043, of which only $1,521,047 were published in the Slave States, and $778,500 in the District of Columbia for the account of the Government. From the statements we have given as to the condition of the Southern population, their capabilities, &c., it is evident that there is but small literary consumption amongst them; most of the above supply is consumed by the people of the Free States.[2]

[1] Mr. Walker's fifth "Letter on American Finances, &c." p. 7.

[2] For statistics, see the *National Almanac*, 1863; Helper's "Impending Crisis;" Mr. Ellison's "Slavery and Secession in America;" "Les Etats-Unis en 1863," &c. &c.

There is another series of facts indirectly bearing on this part of our subject. Vice-President Stephens, in estimating the value of the Union to the South, and in opposing secession, reminded the Georgia Convention, that "The expense of the transportation of the mails in the *Free States* was, according to the Report of the Post-Master General, in 1860, a little more than $13,000,000 while the receipts from those States by the Post-Office Department were $19,000,000. But in the *Slave States* the expenses of this department were $14,716,000, and the receipts only $8,001,026, leaving a deficit of $6,714,974 to be supplied by the North for our accommodation, and without which assistance we must have been cut off from this most essential branch of government." For the first time, perhaps, in the history of the United States, the revenues of the Post-Office Department have been greater than its expenses—and this in consequence of the secession of most of the Slave States.

The South has never had a literature of its own, nor the means of establishing or of conducting any literary enterprise. At a Convention of Delegates from the Slave States, held a few years ago at Savannah, it was a subject of lamentation that "the South had no literature of her own to defend her principles and her rights." One of the delegates stated that the reason of this was that "the publishers at the South could not support the expenditures necessary for the prosecution of any literary undertaking." The same gentleman also assured the Convention that the two principal Southern periodicals—the *Southern Literary Messenger*, and the *Southern Quarterly Review*, the latter edited by Mr. De Bow, were "literally in danger of being abandoned for want of funds." But the South seems to be destitute of the simplest appliances used in book publishing. Thus, a patriotic Charlestonian, desirous of founding a Southern literature, began with the rudiments of knowledge; he prepared a series of books for children, which were carefully expurgated of all taint of abolitionism; nevertheless, he was obliged to have them printed, stitched and bound at the North. Many of the Southern States, also, have had their codes of laws, and the Annual Reports of their Legislatures, printed and published at the North. The *Southern Quarterly Review*, published in New Orleans, is printed and bound in New York. The census of 1850 gives the total number of publishing houses in the Slave States at twenty-four, of which ten were in Maryland; there are more than three hundred in the Free States. These establishments employ 750 paper-mills, with 2,000 engines in constant operation, producing 270,000,000 pounds of paper, valued at $27,000,000, annually (1858-9). Duyckinck's "Cyclopædia of American Literature" states that, of 569 American authors whose places of nativity are given, eighty-seven were natives of the South, and of these most were educated, and many of them became permanent residents, at the North.[1]

The reason of the great inferiority of the South as compared with the North, in everything which relates to education and general intelligence, must be quite obvious; the Southern population, in consequence of slavery, is too poor and too ignorant to maintain or desire a system of common schools. And, as we shall show hereafter, the wealthy and educated classes of the South take no interest in the welfare and improvement of the poorer classes; their interests are diametrically opposite. Consequently nothing is done to supply, by legislative enactments, the educational deficiencies of the people.

Moreover, it has been considered necessary, in the interests of slavery, to place such restrictions upon freedom of speech, freedom of thought, and freedom of the press, at the South, as to prevent any real progress excepting in the extension of "the institution." In most of the Slave States severe laws exist against impugning the right of property in slaves, or against writing, printing, publishing, or speaking, anything which is calculated or intended to bring slavery into disrepute. According to the Louisiana Statutes, this prohibition extends to the intention "to diminish that respect which is commanded to free people of colour for the whites by law, or to destroy that line of distinction which the law has established between the several classes of this community."[2] And these laws are universally made to have a wide range of interpretation and application, so as to include all efforts to enlighten and instruct the community, if by so doing slavery shall be in any way impugned. For instance, Mr. Helper, a native of North Carolina, whose forefathers had been slave-holders in that State, being convinced that slavery was essentially prejudicial to all the best interests of the

[1] Helper, *op. cit.* chap. xii.

[2] Judge Stroud's "Sketch of the Laws relating to Slavery," chap. v.

State and its citizens, wrote a book which none can read without being convinced by the author's arguments; the book contains not a single word addressed to the slaves, nor a word calculated to excite an insurrection, unless it be on the part of the millions of poor non-slaveholding whites, whom Mr. Helper proves to be kept in their ignorant and degraded condition by slavery alone to the exclusive profit of the handful of slave-proprietors. Nevertheless, he was obliged to go to the North to find a publisher. So violent was the hostility which this book excited amongst Southerners, that a Southern Member of the House of Representatives, in the Congress of 1859–60, proposed the following Resolution—"That no person who has endorsed and recommended that book, or the compend from it, is fit to be Speaker of this House." For two months the legislative business of the Government was prevented, because the Southern Representatives, being unable to elect one of themselves, were determined to thwart the election of any anti-slavery man; but at last they were beaten.

Another instance was that of Mr. Hedrick, Professor of Chemistry in the University of North Carolina, who was deposed from his professorship, and compelled to leave the State, simply because, being convinced that slavery was an evil, and an obstacle to progress, he did not hesitate to express his views.[1] Instances of the same sort might be multiplied.

A religious discourse by the late Dr. Channing on West India Emancipation, having been exposed for sale in Charleston, the bookseller was prosecuted by the *South Carolina Association*, and held to bail in the sum of $1,000. The trustees of a college in Alabama, a few years ago, found that Dr. Wayland's book on "Moral Science" "contains abolition doctrine of the deepest dye," and they therefore denounced the said book and forbad its farther use in the institution.[2] De Bow's Review, in one of its numbers published a few years since, condemns "Wayland's 'Moral Science,' and the abolition geographies, readers, and histories, overrunning, as they do, with all sorts of slanders, caricatures, and bloodthirsty sentiments. *They seek to array our children, by false ideas, against the established ordinance of God; and they sometimes take effect.*" None of these books attempt in

[1] Helper, *op. cit.*

[2] Mr. Sumner's "Speech on the Barbarism of Slavery," p. 46.

the least to incite the slaves or the free negroes against the whites, any more than the avowed abolition publications. But it is truth and light which the South has feared to let in upon its white population.[1]

No traveller has visited the Slave States, for years past, who has not been struck with the watchful *espionage* exercised for this object. Mr. Stirling, a Scotsman, wrote, in 1857, "In politics there is no toleration at the South;" and again, "There is a terrorism at work in the Southern States, which effectually keeps down every open expression of dissent from the prevailing orthodox creed of slavery."[2] Charles Mackay, the New York Correspondent of the London *Times*, wrote, in 1859, "The traveller from New England and other Free States no sooner penetrates into the slave-land, than he sees all around him the proofs that slavery is omnipresent. Thought is not free. One may talk of the dissolution of the Union as desirable and probable; one may abuse the President and the ministers, speak ill of Congress and its individual members; one may be profane or immoral in speech; but one must not say a word against the sanctity of the 'peculiar institution.'"[3]

But disgraceful as this system of repression is, the reason for its maintenance is even more so. We have already quoted it as given by Mr. Calhoun's journal,[4]—it is to prevent the consciences of the slave-holders themselves from being disturbed. In the face of the immense social and political influence possessed and unscrupulously exerted by the slave-owners, not only to extend slavery, but also to crush any attempt at enfranchisement of the whites and blacks at home, all hope of change for the better seemed cut off. Mr. Bright well said, "There seemed no way short of a miracle more stupendous than any recorded in Holy Writ, which would in our time, or in a century, have brought about the abolition of slavery in America, but the suicide which the South has committed, and the war it is now waging."

We see thus reduced to their proper value the assertions of those, including the Foreign Secretary of England, who pretend

1 Olmsted's "Journeys and Explorations in the Cotton Kingdom," vol. ii. p. 358.
2 "Letters from the Slave States," pp. 80, 200.
3 "Life and Liberty in America," vol. ii. p. 38.
4 *Ante*, p. 52.

that the restoration of the Union would overthrow the liberty of speech and of the Press, in the Slave States. For thirty years there has been no such liberty at the South, and there never can be under slavery.

Let us now examine into the state of RELIGION at the South.

In the United States, neither the Government of the Union, nor the separate State Governments, are concerned in the support of religion; everything which relates to this important interest is left to the people. And it has not suffered in their hands. We may judge of the comparative estimate in which this matter is held in the two sections of the country, by the liberality with which the various religious institutions and establishments are upheld by the people of each.

The value of the religious edifices in the State of New York alone, in 1850, was $21,539,561 ; in the whole of the Slave States combined of $21,674,581, *i.e.* only $135,020 more; in all the Free States combined the value was $67,773,477. For the printing and circulating of the Bible, the inhabitants of the State of New York contributed $269,447 ; those of the Slave States combined $163,390, although the white population of the latter was more than twice as numerous as of the former. The people of the Free States gave to the funds of the Tract Society $129,590, of the Slave States $39,103. To the various Missionary Societies the people of the Free States contributed $668,123, those of the Slave States $6,924. The Domestic Missionary Society received from the Free States $197,630, from the Slave States the miserable pittance of $270, although the products of their agricultural labour alone were valued at more than $460,000,000 for that year.[1]

The following extract from the *Journal* of a colporteur, employed to visit the poor people of South Carolina, shows the condition in which he found them, as to religious knowledge: "I visited sixty families, numbering 221 souls over ten years of age. Of these only twenty-three could read, and seventeen write. Forty-one families were destitute of the Bible. Average of their attendance at Church, once in seven years. Several persons between thirty-five and forty years of

[1] Helper, *op. cit.* pp. 340, 341.

age had heard but one or two sermons in all their lives. Some grown-up youths had never heard a sermon or a prayer until my visit, and did not know of the Saviour. Boys and girls, from ten to fifteen years old did not know who made them. All the members of one family rushed away to the house of a neighbour when I knelt to pray, begging him to tell them what I meant; others fell on their faces to pray, instead of kneeling."[1]

Now, when it is remembered that South Carolina is one of the oldest of the Slave States, that the planters who control its legislation are the most intelligent and educated of their class, we shall not err, probably, in considering that the religious condition of the white population of that State is a fair sample of that of the other Slave States. The value of the real estate and personal property in South Carolina, in 1850, was $288,257,694; its cotton-crop alone was valued at $9,628,832. And yet not *a cent* was given in that State for the cause of Domestic Missions, in 1850, with its population in such utter destitution of the very means which those missions are intended to supply. In fact it is the *Southern Aid Society*, of New York, which, in connexion with the Domestic Mission Societies of the Northern States, provides, so far as possible, for the necessities of the Southern population.

If the whites of the Slave States be thus destitute of religious knowledge and instruction, what must necessarily be the condition of the Slaves, from whom the law, to a great extent, excludes all possibility of progress in this matter? In most or all of the Slave States, assemblies of the slaves for religious worship or instruction are prohibited between sunset and sunrise, *i.e.* at those hours when, their work in the field being finished, they would have time for assembling themselves together. At no time can the negroes meet excepting in the presence of one or more of the white population. Free negroes are not allowed to preach to slaves, and the latter distrust white preachers.[2]

[1] Olmsted's "Seaboard Slave States," p. 510, quoted from De Bow's *Southern Quarterly Review*, vol. xviii. p. 790.

[2] Mr. Olmsted ("Journeys, &c." vol. ii. p. 227) says that this distrust of the white clergyman, attributed to the slaves, has been generally admitted by all the clergymen at the South with whom he had conversed. He says, "A clergyman of the Episcopal Church, of very frank and engaging manners, said in my presence that he had been striving for seven years to gain the confidence of the small number of Africans belonging to his congregation, and with extreme

In South Carolina the Methodist Conference selected a prudent and discreet person for the express purpose of teaching the slaves. It was his intention, distinctly avowed, to confine himself to verbal instruction. Whereupon a formal remonstrance, signed by more than three hundred and fifty of the leading planters and citizens, was presented to him, as follows: "Verbal instruction will increase the desire of the black population to learn. . . . . Open the missionary sluice, and the current will swell in its gradual onward advance. We thus expect *a progressive system of improvement* will be introduced, or will follow from the nature and force of circumstances, which, if not checked (though it may be shrouded in sophistry, and disguised), *will ultimately revolutionize our social institutions*." The Missionary, of course, withdrew from the field, and the local newspaper, the *Grenville Mountaineer*, stated that "the great body of the people were evidently opposed to the religious instruction of their slaves, even if it were given only orally." [1]

The general rule unquestionably is that religious instruction of the slaves by whites is discouraged. There are, of course, exceptions. Thus, Bishop Polk, of Louisiana, himself the owner of four hundred negroes, and at present a Major-general in the Confederate army, is careful that his slaves shall receive instruction in religious matters, and that all the rites and ceremonies of the Episcopal Church shall be imparted to them at proper times. A still more striking instance of liberality and Christian duty, in this respect, was exhibited by the planters of Liberty County, Georgia, where a Presbyterian clergyman had been employed in

humility he had been lately forced to acknowledge that all his apparent success had been most delusive. When asked how he accounted for this, he at once ascribed it to the negro's habitual distrust of the white race; and, in discussing the causes of this distrust, he asked how, if he pretended to believe that the Bible is the Word of God, addressed equally to all the human race, he could explain to a negro's satisfaction why he should fear to put it directly into the negro's hands, and instruct him to read it and judge for himself of his duty? A planter present, a member of this clergyman's church, immediately observed that these were dangerous views, and advised him to be cautious in the expression of them. The laws of the country, said he, forbade the education of negroes, and the Church was, and, he trusted, always would remain, *the bulwark of the laws*. The clergyman replied that he had no design to break the laws; but he must say that he considered the law which withheld the Bible from the negro unnecessary and papistical in character."

[1] Olmsted's "Journeys, &c." vol. ii. p. 214.

the religious instruction of the slaves, at the expense of their owners. After labouring for thirteen years, with a zeal and judgment which had made him famous, he was called to a professorship of Theology in the University of South Carolina. On retiring from his missionary labours he addressed a valedictory to his late employers on the subject of his recent duties. In this he enumerated some of the chief difficulties which he had had to encounter. These were:—1st, The fact that the slaves are *the property* of their owners. He says, "They are sought after and desired as property, and when possessed must be so taken care of and managed as to be made profitable. . . . Under the influence of the powerful feeling of self-interest, there is a tendency to view and treat them as instruments of labour, as a means of wealth, and to forget, or pass over lightly, the fact that they are what they are, under the eye and government of God. There is a tendency to rest satisfied with very small and miserable efforts for their moral improvement, and to give one's-self but little trouble to correct immoralities and reform wicked practices and habits, should they do their work quietly and profitably, and enjoy health, and go on to multiply and increase upon the earth." "And the slaves," he continues, "feeling and knowing that their masters regard and treat them as their money, *as property only*, are themselves inclined to lose sight of their better character and higher interests; and in their ignorance and depravity to estimate themselves, and religion, and virtue, no higher than their owners do." Again, he says, "One of the chief causes of the immorality of negroes arises from the indifference both of themselves and their owners to family relations. . . . If family relations are not preserved and protected we cannot look for any considerable degree of moral and religious improvement." He finds, also, that the masters overlook too much the habits of thieving practised by the negroes amongst themselves. "While some discipline their people for every act of theft committed against their own interests, they have no care whatever for any amount of pilfering and stealing the people carry on among themselves." He animadverts likewise upon the habits of intemperance which prevail amongst the whites as setting an example to the negroes: "Whatever toleration masters use towards ardent spirits in others, of their own class, they are generally inclined to show none towards their servants; and in effecting this reformation masters and mistresses should set the example."[1]

The general conviction of those who have the best opportunity of judging is that, with a great deal of animal feeling, which assumes the form of religious ecstasy, the slaves are superstitious and ignorant of religious truths to an extraordinary degree. The Rev. C. C. Jones, of Georgia, says that he has "often heard it remarked by men, whose office and standing in the Churches afford them abundant opportunities of observation, that the more they have seen of black members of the Church the less confidence they have been able to place in their religious professions."[2]

Mr. Olmsted gives an interesting account of his visit to "the most profitable estate" he saw. It was situated on a tributary of the Mississippi. The slaves upon it formed about one-twentieth of the whole population of the county, in which the blacks considerably outnumber the whites. They were well cared for materially, and the managers and overseers seemed to be remarkably intelligent and well chosen.

"Being with the proprietor and manager together," writes Mr. Olmsted, "I asked about *the religious condition* of the slaves. There were 'preachers' on the estate, and they had some religious observances on Sundays, but the preachers were said to be the worst characters among them, and, the gentlemen thought, only made their religion a cloak for especial depravity. They were, at all events, the most deceitful and dishonest slaves on the plantations, and oftenest required punishment. The negroes of all denominations, and even those who ordinarily made no religious pretensions, would join together in exciting religious observances. They did not like to have white men preach on the estate, and in future they did not intend to permit them. It excited the negroes so much as to greatly interfere with the subordination and order which were necessary to obtain the profitable use of their labour. They would be singing and dancing every night in their cabins till dawn of day, and utterly unfitted themselves for work."[3] Thus, between

[1] Olmsted's "Journeys, &c." vol. ii. pp. 215—219.

[2] Ibid. p. 225.

[3] Ibid. pp. 193—212.

the two, the negroes had but little chance of receiving any proper religious training; the black preachers were "the most deceitful and dishonest slaves on the plantation," and white preachers were not to be tolerated longer.

When the special correspondent of the *Times* visited the South,[1] he was shown over one of the largest sugar plantations in Louisiana, belonging to an Englishman. He saw the young negroes, and asked one of them, "'Do you know how to read or write?' He evidently did not understand the question. 'Do you go to church or chapel?' A dubious shake of the head. 'Did you ever hear of the Saviour?'—At this moment the overseer interposed, saying, 'I think we had better go on, the sun is getting hot;' and so we rode on gently through the little ones, and when we had got some distance off, the overseer resumed, rather apologetically, 'We do not think it right to put these things into their heads so young, it only disturbs their minds and leads them astray.' Now, in this one quarter," continues the narrator, "there were no less than eighty children, some twelve and some even fourteen years old. No education, no God! their whole life food and play, to strengthen their muscles and fit them for the work of a slave. 'And when they die?' I asked of him. 'Well,' said he, 'they are buried in that field yonder, and some of them have a sort of prayers said over them, I believe.'"

In view of such facts as we have quoted, and which might be multiplied *ad libitum*, is it not a miserable pretence that negro slavery in the United States has been and is "a Providential mode of Christianizing the African?" Even the wretched attempts to accomplish this result, which might have been made a splendid achievement of Christian love, have been so much debased by gross selfishness, as to degrade their authors, for the most part. Thus, for example, Bishop Meade, of Virginia, in a sermon prepared expressly to be read to the slaves, after solemnly assuring them that their very bodies are not their own, but their masters', thus exhorts them: "Pray do not think I wish to deceive you, when I tell you that your masters and mistresses are *God's overseers*, and that, if you are faulty towards them, God Himself will punish you severely for it in the next world, unless you repent of it, and strive to make amends for it, by your

[1] Russell's "Diary, North and South," vol. i. p. 397.

faithfulness and diligence for the time to come, for God Himself hath declared the same," &c. &c.[1]

Can anything be more revolting than to hear a Christian *Bishop* preaching that a man's body is not his own, but the absolute property of another, and comparing the Almighty to a Southern slave-holder? Can anything more completely establish the utter corruption and immoral selfishness of slavery, than this solemn degradation of God Himself to the level of its requirements and policy?

No doubt there are masters and mistresses who would be glad to do their duty to their slaves, in the matter of religious instruction. But the difficulties are too great to be overcome, unless by a combined and determined co-operation of the whole slave-holding population; and such is manifestly out of the question. The wives and daughters of many of the planters do, undoubtedly, devote considerable time to the moral and religious training of their household servants; women are "ministering angels" at the South, as they are elsewhere. But for the training of the plantation slaves, and even of the mass of the poor non-slave-holding whites, almost nothing is done, or is likely to be done. Something more than an angel is needed to roll away the great curse which shuts up the South as a tomb, against the spiritual resurrection of some six or seven millions of human beings, for whom, as yet, Christ hath risen in vain.

Now, this matter of the moral and intellectual training of the slaves is not a mere speculative question in morals or theology. It has a direct and most momentous bearing on the condition of Southern society.

As to the depravation of morals caused by slavery, we have quoted abundant testimony to show what was the prevalent opinion of the early planters. That this effect should have gone on increasing with the increase of slavery, was to have been apprehended. Southerners themselves, in their eagerness to defend their favourite institution, sometimes pretend that its effect is the reverse of injurious on the morals of the white population at the present day. For example, Chancellor Harper, in addressing the Society for the Advancement of Learning, of South Carolina, says, "The tendency of slavery is to elevate the female character, as well as that of the other sex, and for similar

[1] Olmsted's "Seaboard Slave States," pp. 118, 119.

reasons. It would, indeed, be intolerable if, when one class of society is *necessarily degraded,* no compensation were made by the superior elevation and purity of the other."[1]

We submit, in opposition to Chancellor Harper, that it is *primâ facie* improbable that, in a community in which considerably more than one-half of the aggregate population belongs to the class which is "necessarily degraded in respect of moral and intellectual cultivation," as is the case in South Carolina, the remainder should thereby be *elevated.* The tendency of the institution is much more likely to be degrading than elevating to the character of the whites; such was universally admitted to be its tendency, before pecuniary interest had come so completely to pervert the judgment and blind the moral perceptions of Southerners, as it has since. Some acknowledge this to be the result, even now. Thus *The Southern Cultivator*, June, 1855, says, "Could we in all cases trace effects to their real causes, we doubt not but that many young men and women, of respectable parentage and bright prospects, who have made shipwreck of their characters, have been led to take the fatal step by having been exposed, in their early years, to the indelicate and lascivious manners and conversation of their fathers' negroes."[2]

The following acknowledgment is from a lady of Virginia:—"This is one of the great evils hanging over the Slave States, destroying the domestic happiness and the peace of thousands. It is expressed in the single word *amalgamation.* It is not confined to the lower orders of the white population. It pervades the whole Society. Those who indulge in it are to be found amongst all ranks, occupations and professions. . . . I cannot use too strong language in reference to this subject, for I know it will meet with a heart-felt response from every Southern woman."[3]

Now, admitting that at the North society is far from being as virtuous and enlightened as it should be, it is unquestionably vastly more so than at the South. This inferiority of the latter can be traced directly and indirectly to slavery, and to no other cause.

1 Olmsted, "Journeys, &c." vol. i. p. 222.
2 Ibid.
3 "Seaboard Slave States," p. 601.

VI.

THE MATERIAL CONDITION AND PROGRESS OF THE NORTH AND SOUTH COMPARED.

EXAMINED from this point of view, we shall find that slavery has occasioned the same marked contrast between the two sections of the United States as we have shown it to have produced in other respects.

It is important to bear in mind that the two systems of *free-labour* and *slave-labour* began their career at the same time in the United States. The first slaves imported into the colonies were landed on the James River, in Virginia, in 1620, from a Dutch ship. In the same year, "the Pilgrim Fathers" of New England landed on the shores of Massachusetts Bay. We may apply to this notable coincidence the remark made by Louis XVIII. to a courtier who informed him that the Duke of Wellington was born the same year as Napoleon:—"Providence owed us such a compensation."

The area of the nine Free States enumerated in the census of 1790—the first census taken—was 169,668 square miles; of the eight slave-holding States, 300,580 square miles. The population of the former at that time was 1,968,455, of the latter, 1,961,372. But, in 1860, the former had 10,594,168, and the latter 7,414,684, inhabitants; in other words, those Free States have increased their population from 11·60 per square mile, in 1790, to 62·44 in 1860; while the Slave States referred to have increased from 6·52 to 24·66 per square mile, during the same period. No cause, other than slavery, directly and indirectly, can explain this difference in progress in favour of the Free States. For in climate, in salubrity, in abundance of natural resources, the Slave-holding States were far superior to the others. And the shore line, including bays, sounds, rivers, and islands, to the head of tide-water, was for the latter group of States only 4,480 miles against 6,560 miles for the former.[1]

It is very generally stated that the Southern States are so unhealthy to white labourers that negroes are necessary to cultivate the soil. This is a very grievous mis-statement. It is in opposition to the assertions of the best Southern authorities, and is contrary to the testimony of the tables of mortality for the Northern and Southern States compared.

Governor Hammond, of South Carolina, maintained that "the steady heat of our Southern summers is not so prostrating as the short, but frequent and sudden outbursts of heat of Northern summers." Dr. Cartwright, an eminent physician of New Orleans, which is supposed to be the most unhealthy city of the United States, affirms that, "In New Orleans the greater part of the hard labour—work requiring exposure to the sun, such as railway-making, street-paving, cart-driving, the digging of ditches and drains, and house-building—is performed by whites." And he says also, that the country bordering on the lower part of the Mississippi "is exempt from miasmatic fevers, and is extremely healthy." Dr. Barton of New Orleans, confirms his *confrère's* opinion; he thinks that the climate of the South is more favourable to health and vigour than that of the North; that the diseases most common and most fatal at the South are chiefly of a preventible nature. Professor Darby, who surveyed the States of Alabama, Mississippi, Louisiana, and Texas, between the years 1805 and 1815, and who was exposed, with his command, to all the accidents and privations attendant on his occupation, says that they "suffered no sickness of any kind." He adds, "that nine-tenths of the diseases of these warm climates may be prevented, I have no doubt whatever."

A Southern contributor to De Bow's "Resources of the South," vol. ii. p. 43, says, "The cotton-planters, deserting the rolling land, are fast pouring in upon the swamp lands. Indeed, the impression of the sickliness of the South generally has been rapidly losing ground among the whites for some years past, and health is now sought with as much confidence on the swamp-lands of the Yazoo and the Mississippi as among the hills and plains of Carolina and Virginia."[2]

[1] See the third Letter of Hon. R. J. Walker, on "American Finances and Resources," pp. 10, 11. London, 1863: William Ridgway.

[2] Helper, Olmsted, Ellison, *op. cit.*

In 1850, the census report gives the rate of mortality in the seven original Free States as 1 to 68·66 of the entire population; in the six original Slave-holding States as 1 to 78·30. Of the former States, the smallest mortality was in Pennsylvania, 1 to 81·63; of the latter, the smallest was in Georgia, 1 to 91·93. In Florida the mortality was as 1 to 93·67 of the population; in Texas, as 1 to 69·79. The largest mortality in the Free States was in Massachusetts, 1 to 51·23 of the population; in the Slave-holding States, in Louisiana, 1 to 42·85,—not solely owing to the climate, but also to the overtasking of the slaves, especially during the sugar-making season. The general average mortality in all the Free States was as 1 to 73·07 of the aggregate population; in all the Slave States as 1 to 71·81. In the former, the general average was diminished by the extremely low rate in Wisconsin, 1 to 105·82 of the population of that State, and in Vermont, 1 to 100·13 of its inhabitants. Excluding these two, the mortality was lower in the Slave-holding than in the Free States. South Carolina contains more land, the cultivation of which is considered as unfavourable to health, than any other State in the Union; and yet the average mortality in South Carolina, in 1860, was as 1 to 77.22 of its population, while in Massachusetts the rate was as 1 to 60.31.

Now, if we bear in mind that more than half the population of the Slave States are regarded less as human beings (to whom life and health are as dear, and as worthy of preservation and care, as to the whites) than as so much valuable property, and that the number of immigrants, in full vigour and in the prime of youth, is annually very large to the Free States, and very small to the others, we shall be still more struck with the comparative small rate of mortality in the latter as contrasted with the former.

In every one of the Southern States the whites do carry on all sorts of work with as much impunity as the slaves. It is a great stretch of fancy to pretend that any part of that country is uninhabitable by whites. In Alabama, according to the census of 1850, there were 67,742 white males, over fifteen years of age, engaged in agricultural labour; in Mississippi, 50,028; in Georgia, 82,107; in Louisiana, 11,524; in North Carolina, 76,338; in Florida, 5,472. And there is no State at the South in which there are not non-slaveholding whites who till their own small farms, or work for others. In Texas the best cotton-crops are produced by the German population who own no slaves, and their cotton is said to be worth a cent and a half per pound more than the slave-grown.[1]

Thus it is evident that the Slave-holding States are fully as salubrious as the Free States. Consequently their climate opposes no obstacle to white labourers, nor to free black in opposition to slave-labour. They contain all the natural means and aids to material prosperity—navigable streams, good harbours, fertile soils, a genial climate, mineral treasures, wealth-yielding forests—all, excepting gold mines, in far greater profusion than do the Free States. We shall see the comparative use which each section has made of its respective advantages.

We venture to beg the special attention of our English readers to this portion of our argument. One of the great inducements urged upon Englishmen in favour of the Southern rebellion is that, if the South succeeds, a system of direct free-trade will be opened between it and England, which will be so lucrative and advantageous in every way to the latter party, as to far more than counterbalance any probable diminution of traffic between England and the United States. We shall prove the utter fallacy of this argument by showing the miserable condition in which the Southern population is, the small range of its necessities, owing to its low grade of civilization, and its extremely limited means of paying for even the necessities of its existence.

In 1860 the population of the Free States was composed of 19,076,439 whites, and 241,306 blacks, in all, 19,317,745. The Slave-holding States contained 8,199,760 whites, 252,916 free blacks, and 3,952,702 slaves. The Free States embraced 853,953 square miles, 22·62 persons to the square mile; the Slave-holding States 846,632 square miles, 14·65 persons to the square mile.

The States now comprising the Southern Confederacy con-

[1] Helper, *op. cit.* pp. 343—348 ; Ellison, "Slavery and Secession in America," pp 181—184. The unhealthy portion of the South, as compared with the North, s chiefly along some parts of the coast, where fresh and salt water mingle, and produce malaria. But, excluding these lands (on which, so far as cotton is concerned, very little is grown, excepting on the sea-islands, off the coast of Carolina), we have the bottom-lands along the rivers, than which none are more fertile, or, according to Southern accounts, more salubrious, and the great range of upland country perfectly healthy and admirably adapted for cultivation, and furnishing excellent cotton lands.

tained, according to the census of 1860, 5,549,463 white inhabitants, 132,760 free blacks, and 3,520,116 slaves, in all 9,202,339 inhabitants, at an average density of 12·63 to each square mile of territory. The States remaining in the Union contained, according to the same census, 21,726,736 whites, 361,462 free blacks, and 432,586 slaves, in all 22,520,784 persons, representing an average population of 23·16 to each square mile of territory.

In addition, the United States possess of territories not yet admitted as States, but administered by territorial governments under the jurisdiction of Congress, 1,119,226 square miles, with a population of 220,195 inhabitants.[1]

Let us examine into the material condition of each class of the Southern population.

1. The Slave-holding Class.

The number of slaves owned by individuals varies from one to a thousand and upwards. It is stated that, in 1850—55, taking the Slave States in general, there were 68,820 whites who held each but *one* slave; 105,683 from *one* to *five;* 80,765 from *five* to *ten;* 54,595 from *ten* to *twenty;* 29,733 from *twenty* to *fifty;* 6,196 from *fifty* to *one hundred;* 1,479 from *one hundred* to *two hundred;* 187 from *two hundred* to *three hundred;* 56 from *three hundred* to *five hundred;* 9 from *five hundred* to *a thousand;* and 2 held *two thousand* slaves, or more. Mr. De Bow states that the whole number of actual *owners* of slaves was only 186,551; of these proprietors 2,000 were counted more than once, from the fact of their possessing plantations and slaves in different parts of the same State, or in different States; and 158,974 persons *hired* slaves without actually owning them. Thus the whole number of whites employing and directly profiting by slave-labour was, according to this last estimate, but 345,525. It has been a mere handful of men at the South which has governed the United States for nearly a

[1] We have taken our statistics from the *National Almanac* for 1863. The results which we have given differ somewhat from those published by the Hon. R. J. Walker in his "Letters on American Finances and Resources;" but as we have not access to his authorities, we prefer adhering to our own calculations, which anyone can verify.

century, and which has now plunged the country into a civil war because the sceptre was departing from its grasp.[1]

In 1850, the white population of the Slave States was 6,184,477, of which 345,525 held the slaves. Adopting this as about the proportion for 1860, we shall have of the white population at that time (8,199,760), 455,466 holding slaves, and of the white population of the Confederate States (5,549,463), 324,421 slave-holders. During the three years of war which have occurred since, the number has not probably increased very much. Thus, in those States the wealth, (for there slaves are the indication and the standard of wealth, is all concentred in the hands of a very small portion of the population; the non-slaveholders are, for the most part, poor.

The chief crop raised for sale in the Slave States is cotton. The aggregate value of this staple is very great; but it is distributed amongst so many large and small producers, and the expenses attending its production are so considerable, and so large a portion of the proceeds are spent out of the cotton-growing States, that these derive an astonishingly small advantage from it.

The total number of slaves employed in the cultivation of cotton, in 1850, was estimated by Mr. De Bow at 1,800,000, and the aggregate crop at 2,400,000 bales, making an average of *a bale and one-third* for each slave. As a general rule, the smaller the number of slaves on a plantation the less is their average production of cotton. Mr. De Bow estimates that there are 420,000 slaves on plantations owned by planters who work fifty slaves or more each. If these produce on an average only *two and a half* bales of cotton per head (including men, women and children), it will leave an average for the small plantations of *seven-eighths* of a bale per slave. The smaller planters are generally found in the interior, at some distance from a market,—the richer planters having gradually purchased all the more advantageously situated cotton-lands. To the small producer in the interior, who is obliged to pay large costs of transportation to market, and very probably also the expense of cleaning and packing to some wealthier neighbour who possesses the requisite conveniences for this necessary work, his crop is not worth more than an average of *seven cents* per pound, or $30 per bale.

[1] Helper, *op. cit.* pp. 117—120.

Deducting the number of those who hold slaves only as domestic servants from the total number of slave-holders, more than half the latter, and fully one-half of all the cotton-planters, own each not more than one family of, on an average, *five* slaves, of all ages. The ordinary total cash income of one-half of the cotton-planters cannot therefore be estimated at more than $125 per annum, or, in years of unusual productiveness or high prices, $150. With this they must purchase whatever of clothing and other necessaries they may require for the yearly consumption of their own families and their slaves, as well as provide tools and materials requisite to the culture of their land, pay for extra work, if needed, and for professional services, defray taxes, provide education for their children, if any be provided, &c., &c. Hence it is evident that at least one-half of the cotton-planters must be wretchedly poor—poorer than the mass of day-labourers at the North.

A similar calculation will show that those planters who own, on an average, two slave families, or *ten slaves* of all ages, can scarcely produce more than $300 worth of cotton annually. Mr. Olmsted says he has seen "many a workman's lodging at the North, and also in England, where there was double the amount of luxury he ever saw in a cotton-planter's house, on plantations worked by three slave families."

The next class of cotton-planters for whose incomes the census furnishes the materials for an opinion, is that which possesses, on an average, *seven cabins* of five slaves each, including house-servants, the aged and infirm, and children. It is doubtless true that many planters of this class, though by no means all, do obtain handsome returns for their capital.

Planters who possess *ten slave families,* or more, of five slaves each, "have advantages for the cultivation, cleansing, pressing, shipping, and selling of their cotton-crop, by the aid of which they obtain large returns for their investments. The whole number of slave-holders of this class, in all the Slave States, was estimated by Mr. De Bow at 7,929, which comprises all the great sugar, rice, tobacco, and cotton-planters; less than 7,000, certainly, are cotton-planters. A large majority of these live, when they reside on their plantations at all, in districts of which almost the only white population consists of owners and overseers of the same class of plantations. The nearest other whites will be some sandhill vagabonds, between whom and the planters intercourse is neither intimate or friendly."[1]

It is evident, therefore, that the vast majority of the Southern cotton-planters, whose aggregate revenue is so large, have in the average very little money to expend upon anything beyond the merest necessities. And the wealthy, who can afford luxuries, and who are possessed of refinement and education, find themselves compelled to seek, beyond the Slave States, those conditions which refinement and education require for their own gratification and enjoyment, and which no wealth can purchase at home.[2] Moreover, from the sparseness of the Southern population, the character of that population, as a whole, its low grade of civilization, and the very limited range of Southern industry, the larger portion of the aggregate revenue of the planters is necessarily expended abroad in the purchase of a thousand articles for domestic and agricultural purposes, which the South itself cannot furnish. Hence, notwithstanding its apparent wealth, the South is poor, and *the cause of that poverty is, beyond dispute, Slavery.* Furthermore, so long as slavery continues to be the predominant basis of labour, the South must continue to be poor, and hopelessly so.

It is easy to cite Southern testimonies to establish the truth of these statements.

A writer in De Bow's "Industrial Resources," vol. ii., pp. 113, 114, says: "If one unacquainted with the present condition of the south-west were told that the cotton-growing district alone had sold the crop for $50,000,000 annually for the last twenty

[1] See an interesting discussion of this question in Olmsted's "Journeys and Explorations," vol. i. pp. 8—27.

[2] According to the census of 1850, there were more than 600,000 natives of the Slave States residing at the North, while there were less than 100,000 of natives of the Free States living at the South. Mr. Gregg, of South Carolina, says that, of the mercantile class alone, "we shall not have to go much further back than twenty-five years to count up $25,000,000 of capital accumulated in Charleston, and which has left us with its enterprising owners who have located themselves principally in Northern cities. This sum would have built factories enough to spin and weave every pound of cotton grown in the State, besides making railways to intersect every portion of the up-country, giving business facilities to the remotest points." (Olmsted's "Journeys and Explorations," vol. ii. p. 301.) There is, perhaps, not a city or a large town in the middle Atlantic States, and even in Massachusetts, in which there are not Southern families residing permanently, for comfort or for education.

years, he would naturally conclude that this must be the richest community in the world. He might well imagine that the planters all dwelt in palaces, upon estates improved by every device of art, and that their most common utensils were made of the precious metals; that canals, turnpikes, railways, and every other improvement, designed either for use or for ornament, abounded in every part of the land, and that the want of money had never been felt or heard of in its limits. But what would be his surprise when told that, so far from dwelling in palaces, many of these planters live in habitations of the most primitive description, so badly built as to be incapable of protecting their inmates from the wind and rain; that, instead of any artistic improvement, these rude dwellings are surrounded by cotton-fields, or, probably, by fields exhausted, washed into gullies and abandoned; that instead of canals having been constructed, even the navigable streams remain unimproved, to the great injury of commerce; that the common roads of the country are scarcely passable; that the edifices for religious and educational purposes are frequently built of logs and merely roofed with boards; and that the fine arts are but little encouraged or cared-for. . . How would his surprise be increased, when told that instead of being misers and hoarders of money, these planters are generally in want of it, and that many of them are poor and bankrupt."[1]

A very different state of things prevails at the North. Mr. Olmsted well says, "Let a man be absent twenty years from almost any part of the North, and he will be impressed on his return with what are called *the improvements* which have been made — better buildings, churches, school-houses, mills, railways, &c., &c. In New York city alone, for example, at least $200,000,000 have been re-invested merely in an improved housing of the people; in labour-saving machinery, water-works for the supply of the city, gas-works, &c., as much more. It is not difficult to see where the profits of our manufacturers and merchants are. Again, go into the country, and there is no end of substantial proof of twenty years of agricultural prosperity, not alone in roads, canals, bridges, dwellings, barns, and fences, but in books, furniture, gardens, and in the better dress and evidently higher education of the people. But where will the

[1] Cairnes, "The Slave Power," pp. 92–94.

returning traveller find the accumulated profits of the cotton-crops of twenty years in the south-west? Ask the planter for them, and he will point you in reply not to dwellings, churches, school-houses, libraries, mills, railways, or anything of the kind. He will point to his negroes, and to almost nothing else."[1]

This statement of Mr. Olmsted is corroborated in the most forcible language by Mr. T. R. Cobb, of Georgia.[2] "In a slave-holding State," says he, "the greatest evidence of wealth in the planter is the number of his slaves. The most desirable property for a remunerative income is slaves. The best property to leave to his children, and from which they will part with the greatest reluctance, is slaves. Hence the planter invests his surplus income in slaves. The natural result is, that lands are a secondary consideration. No surplus is left for their improvement. The homestead is valued only so long as the adjacent lands are profitable for cultivation. The planter himself having no local attachments, his children inherit none. On the contrary, he encourages in them a disposition to seek new lands. His valuable property (slaves) are easily removed to fresh lands; much more easily than to bring fertilizing materials to the old. The result is that they, as a class, are never settled. Such a population is almost nomadic. It is useless to seek to excite patriotic emotions in behalf of the land of birth, when self-interest speaks so loudly. On the other hand, where no slavery exists, and the planter's surplus cannot be invested in labourers, it is appropriated to the improvement or extension of his farm, the beautifying of the homestead," &c., &c.

This wretched system of exhausting land and then leaving it, alluded to by Mr. Cobb, is prevalent all over the South. We are told in De Bow's "Resources of the South,"[3] that "The native soil of middle Georgia is a rich argillaceous loam, resting on a firm clay foundation. In some of the richer counties nearly all the land has been cleared and appropriated to tillage, a large maximum of which has been worn out, leaving a desolate picture for the traveller to behold,—decaying tenements, red, old hills stripped of their native growth and virgin soil, and washed into deep gullies, with here and there patches of Bermuda peas

[1] "Journeys and Explorations," vol. i. p. 25.
[2] Quoted in Ludlow's "History of the United States," p. 113.
[3] Quoted by Mr. Olmsted, "Seaboard Slave States," p. 533.

and stunted pines struggling for subsistence on what was once one of the richest soils in America."

The Business Committee of the South Carolina State Agricultural Society reported in 1855, "Our old fields are enlarging, our homesteads have been decreasing fearfully in number. . . We are not only losing some of our most energetic and useful citizens to supply the bone and sinew of other States, but we are also losing our *slave population, which is the true wealth of the State;* our stocks of hogs, horses, mules, and cattle are diminishing in size and decreasing in number, and our purses are strained for the last cent to supply their places from the north-western States."[1]

Alabama was admitted into the Union in 1819; in 1855, the Hon. C. C. Clay makes the following remarkable statements concerning its agricultural and material condition: "I can show you with sorrow in the older portions of Alabama, and in my native county of Madison, the sad memorials of the artless and exhausting culture of cotton. Our small planters, after taking the cream off their lands, unable to restore them by rest, manures, or otherwise, are going farther west and south in search of other virgin lands, which they will despoil in like manner. Our wealthier planters, with greater means and no more skill, are buying out their poor neighbours, extending their plantations and adding to their slave force. The wealthy few who are able to live on smaller profits and to give their blasted fields some rest, are thus pushing off the many who are merely independent.

"Of the $20,000,000 annually realised from the cotton-crop of Alabama, nearly all not expended in supporting the producers is re-invested in land and negroes. Thus, the white population has decreased, and the slave population has increased, almost *pari passu,* in several counties of our state. In 1825, Madison county cast about 3,000 votes, now she cannot give more than

[1] Olmsted, "Journeys, &c." vol. ii. p. 292. Mr. Gregg, of Charleston, remarking upon this loss to which South Carolina has been subjected, from the emigration of her citizens, says, "I think it would be within bounds to assume that the *planting* capital withdrawn from the State during the last twenty-five years would, if it had been judiciously applied, have drained every acre of swamp-land in South Carolina, besides resuscitating the old, worn-out land, and doubling the crops—thus more than quadrupling the productive agriculture of the State." (Ibid. 299.)

2,300. In traversing that county, one will discover numerous farm-houses, once the abode of industrious and intelligent freemen, now occupied by slaves, or tenantless, deserted, and dilapidated. He will observe fields, once fertile, now unfenced, abandoned, and covered with weeds. He will see the moss growing on the mouldering walls of once thriving villages; and will find that 'one only master grasps the whole domain' which once furnished happy homes for a dozen white families. Indeed, a country in its infancy, where fifty years ago scarce a forest-tree had been felled, is already exhibiting the painful signs of senility and decay, so apparent in Virginia and the Carolinas. The freshness of its agricultural glory is gone; the vigour of its youth is extinct, and the spirit of desolation seems brooding over it."[1]

A Convention for the organization of the Virginia State Agricultural Society, in 1852, adopted an address which acknowledged the striking retrogression of the State. This paper stated amongst other things: "Whilst our population has increased during the last ten years in the ratio of 11·66 per cent., that of New York has increased 27·52 per cent., and that of Massachusetts at the still higher and more startling ratio of 34·81 per cent. With a wide-spread domain, a kindly soil, a climate whose sun radiates fertility, and whose very dews distil abundance, *we find our inheritance so wasted, that the eye aches to behold the prospect.*"[2]

The same sad picture is drawn of Texas, the most recent and, perhaps, naturally, the richest in soils of the Slave States. Mr. Olmsted (himself a farmer) says, "After two hundred years' occupation of similar soils by a community of free labourers, I have seen no such evidences of waste as I have seen in Texas after ten years of slavery. Waste of soil and injudicious application of labour are common in the agriculture of the North, but nowhere at the North is the land, with what is attached to it, less promising, and less adapted to be the residence of a refined and civilized people now than it was before the opera-

[1] Olmsted, "Journeys, &c." pp. 567—577.

[2] Ibid. pp. 166—170. This Report was once adopted, then re-considered, and again adopted; a second time re-considered, and finally *rejected*, on the ground that "there were admissions in it which would feed the fanaticism of the Abolitionists." Mr. Olmsted quotes almost the whole of this Report in the Appendix to his "Journeys and Explorations," vol. ii. pp. 367—369.

tions commenced which have been attended with the alleged waste." Again, he says, "in Texas, agriculture, with some exceptions among the Germans, is almost as rude and wasteful as it is possible to be. . . . With cotton as the only export, and slaves as the only labourers, no better system will ever be adopted. The growth of wealth is in almost nothing else than slaves, and each crop must go to be capitalized in more labourers. The demand upon the soil being thus incessant, immediate return in quantity, without reference to duration, becomes the measure of success, and must remain so as long as virgin soils are at hand."

In short, it is a matter of notoriety amongst intelligent Southerners, that their country is becoming more and more impoverished. Mr. De Bow says, "Examples may be found in our own country, of States having become poorer in consequence of a steady perseverance in an unwise application of their labour. Such is the case *in all the Atlantic States south of the Potomac*, as I think will be granted by every intelligent and candid individual who is acquainted with the country. I think it will be admitted that these States are even poorer than they were twenty years ago. There is a small increase in the number of labourers, and there may have been something gained in skill; *but the great source of all wealth in an agricultural country, the soil, has been greatly deteriorated and exhausted.*" [1]

Not only are intelligent Southerners aware of the growing deterioration of their land under slave-labour, but the superiority of free-labour has been often exhibited, under circumstances which have rendered doubt impossible. Thus, to give one example out of many: in Fairfax County, Virginia, the result of the comparison is given in the following words, from the Agricultural Report of the Commissioner to the Patent Office in Washington. "In appearance, the country is so changed that a traveller who passed over it ten years ago would not now recognise it. Thousands and thousands of acres, which had been cultivated in tobacco by the former proprietors, and would not pay the cost, were abandoned as worthless, and became covered with a wilderness of pines. These lands have been purchased by Northern emigrants, the large tracts have been divided and cleared of pines, and neat farm-houses and barns, with smiling

[1] Cairnes, *op. cit.* p. 85.

fields of grain and grass, in the season, salute the delighted gaze of the beholder. Ten years ago it was a mooted question whether Fairfax lands could be made productive, and, if so, would they pay the cost. This problem has been satisfactorily solved, and, in consequence of the altered state of things, *school-houses and churches have doubled in number.*"[1]

As to the amount and kind of success which the South has achieved under the *régime* of slavery, during the two centuries and-a-half of its career, we may sum it up as follows: It has rapidly and effectually exhausted its naturally rich soil of all those elements which are most easily extracted from it, and it has almost completely neglected all the other natural resources of the country. Moreover, by proscribing manufactures and commerce; by limiting agricultural operations within narrow bounds, and to an ignorant and degraded class of labourers; by preventing white immigration; by rendering the formation of an intelligent, industrious, and thriving middle-class impossible; by virtually interdicting any system of common-school education; by these and similar means, slavery has succeeded in enriching a very small number of slave-holders, at the expense of the civilization and prosperity of the millions of the white inhabitants of the South, and in limiting, so far as possible, by legislation and neglect, the advantages which might have accrued to the slaves from their association with the dominant race.

In some districts there are, as we have seen, considerable numbers of small farmers, who possess no slaves, and who carry on comparatively limited agricultural operations with their own hands, aided sometimes by hired white labour. But these farmers are generally looked upon with dislike and suspicion by the slave-holders, as well as by the great masses of the poor whites. They cannot compete with the wealthier planters, and are, consequently, becoming more and more poor. Their small farms are continually being purchased by their richer neighbours, and they themselves go elsewhere to commence upon fresh soils the process of waste and ruin.

As to the planters and their families, we find the following, amongst the statements made concerning their habits and mode of living, which will interest those who think that free-trade with them will conduce much to the profit of English manu-

[1] Cairnes, *op. cit.* p. 213.

facturers. Of course, we are not unaware that all over the Slave States, and especially in the older, there are planters who will compare favourably in point of intelligence, refinement, and breeding with their compeers in wealth of any country. But these are manifestly exceptions to the generality of their class.

Mr. Olmsted, who has visited the Slave States on several occasions—and who has passed, if we are not mistaken, about two years therein—speaks of having visited "planters, who not only did not themselves enjoy, but who have never imagined, or aspired to, a tithe of the comfort to which most journeymen mechanics, whom I have known, are habituated—gentlemen, nine-tenths of whose neighbours, for a hundred miles around them, live in a manner which, if witnessed at the North, would make them objects of compassion to the majority of our day-labourers."

He says that, in his last journey of nearly three months between the Mississippi and the Upper James River, in Virginia, in nine cases out of ten he was obliged to sleep in a room with others, in a bed which stank, supplied with but one sheet, if any; to wash with utensils common to the whole family. He found no garden, no flowers, no fruit, no tea, no cream, no sugar, no bread (but *corn-pone*); no curtains to the windows; three times in four absolutely no windows; no hay, nor straw, nor oats, for his horse, &c. &c. "In nine-tenths of the houses south of Virginia," says he, "in which I was obliged to spend the night—making all reasonable endeavours to find the best—there were none of these things. Most of these houses had been recommended to me, by disinterested persons on the road, as being better than ordinary. From the banks of the Mississippi to the banks of the James, I did not see (that I remember), excepting perhaps in one or two towns, a thermometer, nor a copy of Shakespeare, nor a piano, nor a sheet of music, nor the light of a carcel or other good centre-table or reading-lamp, nor an engraving, nor copy of any kind of a work of art of the slightest merit. I am not speaking of 'poor whites;' a large majority of all these houses were the residences of slave-holders, a considerable proportion of them cotton-planters." [1]

Again, he says, "As I think of the houses into which I have had glimpses, in Virginia, it does not seem to me that men who

[1] "Journeys and Explorations," vol. ii. pp. 280—286.

are reputed to be worth $400,000 have equal advantages of wealth with those who possess one quarter of that amount in the Free States. Men with $40,000 live not so well here as men worth $10,000 at the North. The farmer who owns half-a-dozen negroes, and who, I suppose, must be worth $4,000, does not approach, in his possession of civilized comfort, the well-to-do working-man at the North, who rents a small house, and whose property consists in its furniture, his tools, skill, and strength, and a few hundred dollars laid up in the Savings' Bank." [1]

An intelligent man, who had travelled two years in Louisiana, having business with the planters, described the condition of most of the new slave-holders and the small planters as being "very miserable." He had sometimes found it difficult to get food at their houses, even when he was in urgent need of it. "The majority of the wealthy Creole planters," he said, "do nothing to improve their estates, and are very apt to live beyond their income. The majority of all planters, he thought, would always run in debt to the extent of their credit, for the purchase of negroes, whatever price might be asked for them, without ever making any calculation as to the reasonable prospect of their being able to pay their debts. When any one made a good crop he always expected that his next would be still better, and made purchases of slaves in advance upon such expectations." Comparing the condition of people of property in New York and Louisiana, he said, "that, with some rare exceptions, farmers worth $40,000 in New York lived in greater comfort and enjoyed more refined and elegant leisure than planters in Louisiana worth $300,000; and that farmers of the ordinary class in New York, who laboured with their own hands, and were worth some $6,000, lived in far greater comfort and in all respects more enviably than planters worth $50,000 in Louisiana. He might travel many days, and call upon a hundred planters, and hardly see in their houses more than one newspaper, perhaps not one; nor any books, excepting a Bible, and some Government publications which had been franked to them through the Post-office, and perhaps a few religious tracts, or school-books." [2]

1 "Journeys and Explorations," vol. i. p. 137.

2 Ibid. vol. ii. pp. 44—48.

"In our whole journey through Eastern Texas," says Mr. Olmsted,[1] "we did not see one of the inhabitants look into a book or a newspaper, although we spent days in houses where men were lounging about the fire without occupation. . . . We stopped one night at the house of a planter, now twenty years settled in Texas. He was a man of some education and natural intelligence; and had, he told us, an income of $4,000 from the labour of his slaves. His residence was one of the largest houses we had seen in Texas. Its windows had once been glazed; but now, out of eighty panes that once filled the lower windows, thirty only remained unbroken. Not a door of the house had ever been furnished with a latch, or even a string; when a door was closed it was necessary to *claw* it, or to ask some one inside to push it, open. The furniture was of the rudest description," &c. &c.

As to the amount of comfort and elegance in the style of living of the Alabama planters, Mr. Olmsted says, "Much the larger portion of the planters of this State live in *log-houses*, some of them very neat and comfortable, but frequently rude in construction, the spaces between the logs not stopped, the windows unglazed, and altogether wanting in many of the commonest conveniences possessed by the poorest class of Northern farmers and labourers of the older States. Many of those who live in this way possess considerable numbers of slaves, and are every year buying more. Their early frontier life seems to have destroyed all capacity to enjoy the usual luxuries of civilized life." [2]

Such are, for the most part, the members of the boasted *Southern Aristocracy*, to which the aristocracy of England holds out the right hand of fellowship. It is now, as a body, as Howison described it a century ago in Virginia, "An aristocracy neither of talent, nor of learning, nor of moral worth, but of landed and slave interest." Its wants—such as England will, with any probability, be called on to supply—are few; its tastes and habits unrefined; and its aspirations pretty much limited to cotton, and to negroes as producers of cotton.

[1] "Journeys and Explorations," pp. 9—11.
[2] Ibid. pp. 575, 576.

2. The Non-Slaveholding Whites.

Professor Cairnes, in the Appendix to his admirable book on "The Slave Power," has made some interesting approximate calculations as to the numbers and general condition of this large class of the Southern population.

The owners of five slaves or more are generally rated as *planters;* those who hold fewer slaves are called *farmers.* In 1850 there were in all the Slave States 173,022 planters, so called. Now, inasmuch as it is by no means uncommon for a planter to own two or more plantations, we may safely assume that these 173,022 planters owned at least 200,000 estates. The whole number of plantations and farms in the Slave States was, according to Colton's Atlas, in 1850, 373,106; deducting from this number the above 200,000, we shall have remaining 173,106 for the rest of the white population of the South, not included under the denomination of planters.

The whole number of white families in the Slave States, in 1850, was 1,114,687, from which if we subtract the planters' families as above, there remain 941,665 other white families, and only 173,106 farms. Now the chief interest and occupation at the South is agricultural.

In the slave-holding States, as at the North, the small farmers usually possess only so much land each as can be cultivated by the members of their own families; if the holdings are larger, the farmers find it more advantageous to hire slave-labour than to employ such indifferent and uncertain white-labour as the country affords.[1] Consequently, the number of non-slaveholding and non-landholding whites engaged in agricultural operations is small. It will be a liberal estimate which assumes that each of the 173,106 farms furnishes employment to one-fourth of a poor white family, which would make the whole number of white persons occupied in agricultural employments, including the families of the farmers themselves, 1,244,289 (216,382 families), taking the census average as to the numbers composing the families. That this estimate is ample is evident from the fact that, according to the census of 1850, the whole number of whites over fifteen years of age engaged in agriculture was only

[1] Olmsted, Stirling, &c. &c.

803,052.[1] The majority of the whites thus engaged in farming are found in the western part of Virginia, the eastern part of Tennessee, in Kentucky, some portions of North Carolina and Alabama, and in Texas. Thus, deducting these 216,382 families from the 941,665 to be provided for, we have remaining 725,283, comprising, according to the census average, 4,170,687 persons, to be supported by some other than agricultural labour.

The above figures refer to the census of 1850. But, during the subsequent ten years, the white population of the Slave States had increased from 6,222,418 to 8,199,760. Increasing in the same proportion, the white population not occupied in agriculture has augmented from 4,170,687 to 5,496,635. If we confine our observations to the poor non-slaveholding whites of the Confederate States, we shall have, according to the population elsewhere given, at least 3,731,821 in that section who gain their livelihood by other than agricultural employments.

We know that the manufacturing industry of the slave-holding States employs but few labourers; in 1860, according to the census, there were 110,110 persons so employed in the Confederate States, and of these many were slaves. The mercantile marine is very small, and can give occupation but to few persons. Three-fourths, at least, of the men employed in navigating the canals and rivers are said to be Irish and Germans; the remainder are slaves; the poor whites are so averse to labour that they cannot be relied upon for continued engagements. In the Southern cities and towns, the servants at hotels, the ordinary workmen, the mechanics and artisans, are foreigners or slaves; the servants in private families are slaves, of course, or foreign whites in rare cases. In the vast pine-forest districts, the great majority of the men employed are slaves.

All over the Slave States game is so abundant, even in the vicinity of towns, that by hunting and fishing an ample supply of animal food can be obtained. Moreover, the comparative mildness of the climate renders clothing a less expensive article of supply than at the North, and fuel is everywhere abounding. Hence diminished incentives to labour.[2]

Consequently, after deducting from the gross number, 3,731,821,

[1] Helper, *op. cit.* p. 343.

[2] Mr. Olmsted and Mr. Stirling, in their several works, give abundant testimony as to the general idleness of the poor whites at the South.

all who are likely to be occupied in other than agricultural pursuits, we shall have left not less than 3,000,000 avowed and systematic idlers in the Confederate States of America, or *more than one-half their total white population.*

And the reason of this gigantic evil is simply that labour has been made the duty and badge of slavery, and the poor whites are too proud to assume them. Hence almost all the attempts hitherto made to establish manufactories at the South have failed; the poor native whites will not work in them, and the planters are so afraid of the influence of immigrant whites that there is little or no encouragement offered to such; they are spoken of as "a curse instead of a blessing, generally a worthless, unprincipled class, *enemies to our peculiar institution,* and formidable barriers to the success of our native mechanics." So says *The South Carolinian.*[1] And here is just the difficulty; the "*peculiar institution*" is an enemy to the poor native whites, whom it degrades, and to foreign operatives whom it fears and suspects.

The testimony of Southerners themselves as to the wretched condition and prospects of the millions of poor whites is unmistakably confirmative of our assertions with regard to them.

A Southerner, who had resided many years in South Carolina, and who had also visited Mexico, speaking to Mr. Olmsted of extensive communities on the banks of the Congaree, in Carolina, used the following language: "They are the descendants of the former proprietors of nearly all the land of that region; but for generations their fathers have been gradually selling off to the richer planters, moving in among them, and living upon the purchase-money of their lands. Their children have been brought up in listless, aimless idleness, more destructive to them as a people than even forced and servile industry might have been. They are more ignorant, their superstitions are more degrading, they are much less enduring and industrious, far less cheerful and animated, and very much more incapable of improvement and elevation, than the most degraded *pæons* of Mexico. Their chief sustenance is a porridge of cow-peas, and the greatest luxury with which they are acquainted is a stew of bacon and peas with red pepper, which they call *Hopping-John.*"[2]

Mr. Wm. Gregg, of Charleston, in a lecture delivered before

[1] Quoted by Mr. Olmsted, "Seaboard Slave States," p. 511.

[2] Ibid. pp. 505, 506.

the South Carolina Institute, in 1851, says, "From the best estimates that I have been able to make, I put down the white people who ought to work, but do not, or who are so employed as to be wholly unproductive to the State, at 125,000." The whole white population of South Carolina in 1850 was only 274,563. Mr. Gregg continues: "Any man, who is an observer of things, could hardly pass through our State without being struck by the fact that all the capital, enterprise, and intelligence are employed in directing slave-labour. The consequence is, that a large proportion of our poor white people is wholly neglected, and suffered to waste existence in a condition only one step above that of the Indian of the forest."[1]

Governor Hammond, of South Carolina (in 1850), says of this class of its inhabitants, "Their industry, such as it is, and compensated as it is, is not, in the present condition of things, *and does not promise hereafter to be,* adequate to procure them, honestly, such a support as every white person in this country feels himself entitled to. Some cannot be said to work at all. They obtain a precarious subsistence by occasional jobs, by hunting, fishing, sometimes by plundering fields or folds, and too often by what is, in its effects, far worse—trading with slaves, and seducing them to plunder for their benefit."[2] And in another part of the same address, Governor Hammond affirms that "$18, or at most $19, will cover the whole necessary annual cost of a full supply of wholesome and palatable food, purchased in the market." Now, what a degraded, demoralised condition must this large population be in (according to Governor Hammond's estimate more than one-sixth, according to Mr. Gregg's almost one-half, the total white population of the State), which is willing to live habitually in the disgraceful way pointed out by Governor Hammond, rather than condescend to earn, by honest labour, the insignificant sum of $19 annually. And this under the government of the *crème de la crème* of Southern aristocracy in South Carolina!

Mr. Tarver, of Missouri, writing of the same class in that State, says, "The non-slaveholders possess, generally, but very small means, and the land which they own is almost universally poor, yielding but a very scanty subsistence. The more fertile

[1] Helper, *op. cit.* p. 404.

[2] Olmsted's "Journeys," &c. vol. ii. p. 294.

soil is in the hands of the slave-holders, and must always remain so. This condition of things depresses the energies of the poorer people. . . And I lament to say that I have observed, of late years, an evident deterioration taking place in this part of the population—the younger being less educated, less industrious, and in every way less respectable than their ancestors."[1]

Of the poor white population of the pine districts, Mr. Olmsted says, "The negroes are decidedly superior to them in every intellectual and moral respect. Among them is a large number, I should think a majority, entirely uneducated, poverty-stricken, and vagabond—I mean people without habitual, definite occupation, or reliable means of livelihood. They are poor, having almost no property but their own bodies; and the use of these, that is their labour, they are not accustomed to hire out statedly and regularly, so as to obtain capital by wages, but only occasionally by the day or job, when driven thereto by necessity. A family of these people will commonly hire, or '*squat*' and build, a little log cabin, so made that it is only a shelter from rain, the sides not being *chinked*, and having no more furniture nor pretension to comfort than is commonly provided for a criminal in the cell of a prison. They will cultivate a little corn, and possibly a few roods of potatoes, beans, &c. They will own a few swine, that find their own food in the forest, and certainly a rifle and dogs. The men profess to spend most of their time in hunting."[2]

The following is written by a gentleman, whose name, says Mr. De Bow, "has long been illustrious for the services he has rendered to the South:"—"All of you must be aware of the condition of the class of people I allude to. What progress have they made in the last hundred years? and what is to be their future condition, unless some mode of employment be devised to improve it? A noble race of people! reduced to a condition but little above the wild Indian of the forest, or the European gipsy, without education, and in many instances unable to procure the food necessary to develop the natural man. They seem to be the only class of people who are not disposed to emigrate to other States, while our wealthy and intelligent citizens are leaving us by scores, taking with them the treasures accumulated

[1] Helper, *op. cit.* p. 130.

[2] Olmsted, "Seaboard Slave States," pp. 348, 349.

by mercantile thrift, as well as by the growth of cotton, and the consequent exhaustion of our soil."[1] This destitution prevails in an agricultural country, where land is of a fabulous cheapness, and where labour is so scarce that the cotton-planters cannot supply the demand for their great staple, so that, in their estimation, it is absolutely necessary to re-establish the African slave-trade; and where, too, "wholesome and palatable food may be purchased, in the market," at the rate of five cents a day, or less, for each grown person.

This is the population which Governor Adams, of South Carolina, pronounced "hopelessly doomed to ignorance, poverty and crime;" which Mr. Lumpkin, of Georgia, characterized as "poor, degraded, half-fed, half-clothed, and ignorant—without Sabbath-schools, or any other kind of instruction, mental or moral, and without any just appreciation of character."

The poor whites have never been regarded with favour by the planters. General Marion, South Carolina, said of them, almost a hundred years ago, "The poor here are very poor, because, not being necessary to the rich, who have their slaves to do all their work, they get no employment." Other reasons are given by Governor Hammond, in the quotation we have made a few pages before, viz.:—they are idle, adverse to labour, and, consequently, being without any intellectual and moral training, immoral and dishonest; and their example has a bad effect upon the slaves. Hence, as we have seen, the planters are constantly endeavouring to accomplish the removal of this class from the vicinity of their plantations, by purchasing the surrounding land.

But another reason for the dislike of the planters towards this class is, the consciousness that their interests are dissimilar and antagonistic; for the poor whites can have no possible interest in the maintenance of slavery; on the contrary, this institution is the prolific cause of all their poverty and degradation. Hence they are looked upon with a certain fear by the slaveholders. De Bow's *Review* for January 1850,[2] revealed this apprehension as follows: "The great mass of our poor white population is beginning to understand that they have *rights*, and that they also are entitled to some of the sympathy which should fall upon the suffering. They are fast learning that there is an

[1] Olmsted, "Journeys," &c. vol. ii. pp. 293, 294, quoted from De Bow.

[2] Quoted by Mr. Olmsted, "Journeys," &c. vol. ii. p. 357.

almost infinite world of industry opening before them, by which they can elevate themselves and their children from wretchedness and ignorance to comfort and intelligence. *It is this great upheaving of our masses that we have to fear*, so far as our peculiar institutions are concerned." Hence, the Legislatures of the Southern States, under the sway of the slaveholders, have done as little as possible, as we have seen, to elevate and educate this population. For with education would come the perception of the wrongs inflicted upon them, and of the true cause thereof, together with the intelligence and the power to right themselves.

This class has always been made use of by the wealthy and intriguing schemers of the South. It furnished the recruits for the Cuban and Central American expeditions, and one can readily understand how easily it has been led to co-operate in the slaveholders' rebellion. Fighting as regular soldiers is a much more respectable avocation than any it has ever been engaged in in peace; the men are brave, and accustomed to regard the planters as their natural rulers; having nothing but their lives to lose, the prospect of gain by the war, the excitements of military life, and the lure held out to them that, Southern independence gained, the African slave-trade will be re-opened, and every white man become a slaveholder at small cost—these were inducements more than enough to gain their hearty concurrence. The present war will, if anything can, convince the poor whites who survive it that their great enemy is not *Northern Abolitionism,* as the slave-owners have taught them to believe, but *the peculiar institution;* and that their only hope of ever being able to enter the promised land—" the infinite world of industry,"—lies in the abolition of slavery. Nothing save this can ever accomplish, or render possible, the regeneration of this the largest class of the Southern population.

It appears to us, then, that the white population of the South —slave-holders and non-slaveholders—offers but a very sorry prospect to the English manufacturing and commercial classes. And so long as the labour-system of the Confederacy is a servile one, independence can only make it less promising, because society will become more of a slaveocracy than before, and the evils of slavery will become more pervading and more unmitigated. What few seeds of opposition to slavery it may have contained previously will infallibly be destroyed by the very success of the attempt to uphold and perpetuate the system. The poor whites will have been swept away by scores of thousands; the small farmers will have been ruined, and the triumphant planters will be left amidst their wretched slaves and the havoc and desolation of the war. No imagery so well depicts this result of the conflict as that employed by Milton to describe the scene disclosed to Satan when, hurled "with hideous ruin and combustion" from heaven, which he had endeavoured to infect with his crime, he awoke to a full sense of his condition, where

> "Darkness visible
> Served only to discover sights of woe,
> Regions of sorrow, doleful shades, where peace
> And rest can never dwell, hope never come."

3. The Slaves.

Much has been written to prove, as some compensation for the admitted evils of slavery, that the *material condition*, at least, of the slaves is far better than that of the mass of the labouring population of Europe, or of the Free States of the American Union. Even in the country of Wilberforce and Clarkson, the *philosophers* of the *Saturday Review* and the *Times* school have argued that "there is, after all, but little essential difference between the condition of a slave, who is supported by his master in exchange for his labour, and that of a free man, who is obliged to expend the wages which he receives for his work in supporting himself and his family."

We admit that the slaves at the South are sufficiently provided with the mere necessaries of life, even when, from age, infirmity, or sickness, they cannot labour for their masters. But, from the very relationship of master and slave, this material well-being is uncertain, and subject to contingencies over which certainly the slave, and often the master, has no control—caprice, passion, cruelty of disposition, ignorance, faults of overseers, death of the owner, and sale of the slave. Even self-interest, which, we are told, will generally secure good treatment and proper support for the black, is a broken reed for him to lean upon: in Cuba it has not prevented the slaves from being worked to death in the ratio of from 3 per cent. to 7 per cent. per annum beyond their increase.[1] In our own slaveholding States, where the greater cost of slaves, as compared with Cuba, makes their lives and vigour objects of more consequence to their owners, they are often overworked and maltreated shamefully.[2] But the fact that the slave cannot be sure of receiving even mere material good treatment is evident from this, that he cannot claim his own person as his own; it may be sold, whipped, and otherwise maltreated by the sanction even of the law.

It is worth while to inquire, what is the amount of material care which the slaveholders afford to their slaves. In sickness they are medicated by the overseer or by a physician; they are housed, clothed, and fed.

As to the food of slaves.—In North Carolina the law of 1753 did order that "*a quart of corn per day*" should be provided as the food of a slave; but the Revised Statutes of 1836-37 substituted for this specification the vague term "*properly fed.*" In Louisiana, an Act of 1806 directs that "every owner shall be held to give to his slaves *one barrel of Indian corn,* or the equivalent thereof in rice, beans, or other grain, *and a pint of salt,* and to deliver the same to the said slaves in kind, *every month,* and never in money, under a pénalty of $10 for every offence." It also ordains that, as clothing, each slave "shall be entitled to receive from his owner one linen shirt and pantaloons for the summer, and a linen shirt and woollen great-coat and pantaloons for the winter." The other slave-holding States do not pretend to fix the amount or kind of food or clothing, but direct that it shall be *proper, sufficient,* &c.[3] But it must be borne in mind that in no slave-holding State is a negro's testimony, whether slave or free, admitted against a white man; consequently, the

[1] Statement of the British Consul in Cuba, quoted by Mr. Stirling, "Letters from Slave States," p. 109.

[2] Mr. Stirling quotes, from De Bow's *Review*, the Report of a Committee of Slave-holders, the admission that "as the only aim of the overseers, in general, is to get the largest possible crop for the year, we can readily conceive the strong inducement they have to overwork our slaves; and masters are often much to blame for encouraging this feeling in their overseers." Ibid. p. 290. Mr. Wirt, in his day, characterized this class of persons as "last and lowest, most abject, degraded, unprincipled," &c.

[3] Judge Stroud's "Sketch of the Laws relating to Slavery," pp. 46—65.

slave can have no legal redress against, nor can he establish (excepting by evidence of starvation or suffering) the fact of insufficiency of food or clothing.

We believe that as a general rule the amount and variety of food given to the slaves is greater than the above legal enactments require, and that pork is usually allowed in some form, three pounds per week being the largest allowance for an adult field slave.

In a document presented to the United States Government in 1846, and signed by forty-eight sugar-planters of Louisiana, the cost of clothing and feeding a working slave was stated at $30 per annum; of clothing alone, at from $10 to $15 annually. The cost of food is greater in Louisiana than in any other slave-holding State, because but little corn is raised there. A planter of South Carolina, in the same document, estimated the total annual expense of both food and clothing at only $15 per slave.[1]

Now what labouring man in the Free States contents himself with food which costs only 5½ cents—less than 3d., per day? The lowest price paid by agricultural labourers in the Free States is 21 cents daily for their board; the majority of labourers pay, probably, twice as much. For years past labourers in those States have received from $1 to $1.75 per day, as wages, according to their labour and skill. Consequently there is no one who, if he be industrious and well-disposed, is not able not only to provide for himself and his family far better materially than any slave is provided for, but also to set aside something against emergencies, or to lay the foundation of competency and even wealth.

Moreover, the duration of the daily task of the slave is far greater than that of the free labourer. In most of the slave-holding States the law is silent as to the number of hours which the slave shall labour. In South Carolina the Code fixes *fourteen* hours daily during six months of the year, and *fifteen* hours during the remainder, as the legal task. The other States forbid *excessive* labour. In Louisiana, during the sugar-making season, eighteen hours daily is the common day's work. But the law which forbids his testimony renders more or less nugatory any attempt to limit the overtasking of the slave. The Supreme Court of Alabama has given legal validity to the custom which

[1] Quoted by Mr. Olmsted, "Journeys," &c.

prevails in cases of real or pretended sickness of the slave, as follows :—"The master or owner, and not the slave, is the judge whether the slave be too sick to labour. The slave cannot therefore resist the order of the master or owner to go to work."[1]

In the Free States, nowhere is the legal or customary day's work over *ten hours ;* if any man voluntarily works beyond that time he is paid in proportion.

But there are other elements in the *material* fate of the slave which, one would suppose (as all Northern Americans did suppose, until within the last three years), would make any honest Englishman—nobleman, scholar, statesman, merchant, manufacturer, or what not—ashamed, for any paltry motive of policy, or gain, to advocate the cause of the Government which avowedly upholds the system of slavery. John Locke long ago characterized it as "the state of war continued between a lawful conqueror and his captive,—so opposite to the generous temper and courage of our nation, that 'tis hardly to be conceived that an Englishman, much less a gentleman, should plead for it."

A slave has no *rights* whatever. Judge Wardlaw, of South Carolina, has decided that "every endeavour to extend to a slave *positive rights* is an attempt to reconcile inherent contradictions ; for, in the very nature of things, he is subject to despotism."[2]

He has no right of ownership over his own body ; he can be sold whenever the necessity or the caprice of his owner may direct his sale. A *Church* in South Carolina sold a slave to purchase a piece of plate for the communion-table.[3]

He has no *right* to the proceeds of his own labour, even over and above that which by the master's consent may be due to the said master ; if, with the latter's permission, the slave shall gain any thing *in compensation of this extra labour,* the slave can establish no claim to it. There are many judicial decisions in point. The following case occurred in 1846 : "The plaintiff's slave, William, made money over and above his wages, and placed it in the hands of the defendant to aid in purchasing his (William's) children. The children were accordingly purchased by the defendant. The Court held that the plaintiff was entitled to recover the money from the defendant. Notwithstanding *any*

1 Judge Stroud, *op. cit.* pp. 39—46.

2 Ibid. p. 34.

3 Senator Sumner's "Speech on the Barbarism of Slavery," p. 42.

promise by the master that his slave shall have certain acquisitions, all the acquisitions of the slave in possession are the property of his master." A slave cannot by law hire himself out to labour, even by the consent of his master; the master is liable to a fine who permits it. In Mississippi no slave can cultivate cotton for his own use, under penalty of a fine against the master. Slaves cannot possess property by devise, descent, or purchase.[1]

In the abstract, can anything be more mean than that one man, in exchange for *the merest modicum* of material support necessary to sustain life and vigour, should seize and appropriate to himself all the labour of another, his equal before God, the sum of which far outvalues the compensation given? Does it not realize the description by the poet of that charitable individual who

> "With one hand put
> A penny in the urn of poverty,
> And with the other took a shilling out?"

A slave can make no contract of any kind, not even of marriage. The relationship formed between slaves, to which the term *marriage* is conventionally applied, has no sanctity, neither are any civil rights attached to it. "A slave has never maintained an action against the violator of his bed. A slave is not admonished for incontinence, or punished for fornication or adultery; never prosecuted for bigamy, or petty treason for killing a husband being a slave, any more than admitted to an appeal for murder." The Supreme Court of North Carolina decided "that a slave, who was the wife of another slave, might give evidence against him, even in a capital case." The law does not prevent (however in some instances and in certain societies custom or sentiment may oppose) the forced separation, by sale or otherwise, of man and wife, or parent and child, thus violating two of God's own laws almost as ancient as the creation.[2]

The master may inflict, or authorize to be inflicted, upon his slave, almost any kind or amount of punishment he may deem fit. The law and public opinion do indeed secure, to a great degree, the slave against loss of life, and, as it is considered in the Slave States, dreadful cruelty, from his master or his

[1] Judge Stroud, *op. cit.* pp. 74—81.
[2] Ibid. p. 99.

K

master's representative. But here, as in other cases, the law which refuses to receive a negro's testimony against either, throws the door wide open to great abuses. And the authors of atrocities such as no other codes would tolerate or palliate, are subjected only to pecuniary fines in many of the Slave States of America. Thus the Act of 1740, of South Carolina—"the purest in its slave condition," as one of her present distinguished men styles it—contains a provision which, according to Judge Stroud, has never been repealed, to this effect: "In case any person shall wilfully cut out the tongue, put out the eye, castrate, or cruelly scald, burn, or deprive any slave of any limb or member, or shall inflict any other cruel punishment, other than by whipping or beating with a horsewhip, cowskin, switch, or small stick, or by putting irons on, or confining or imprisoning such slave, every such person shall, for every such offence, forfeit the sum of *one hundred pounds* current money."[1] A cruel feature in the spirit of the law is that, not only cannot a slave testify against his master, but the latter is almost always befriended by the law. Thus we find a judicial decision of a court in Virginia declaring, "*It is the policy of the law,* in respect to the relation of master and slave, and for the sake of securing proper subordination and obedience on the part of the latter, *to protect the master* from prosecution, even if the whipping and punishment be malicious, cruel, and excessive."[2] The Supreme Court of North Carolina has even decided that "the *hirer* of a slave cannot be indicted for 'a cruel and unreasonable battery' on such slave."[3]

Slaves cannot redeem themselves, nor obtain a change of masters, though cruel treatment may have rendered such change necessary for their personal safety. This is true of all the States as to the non-possession of the right of redemption. In Louisiana and Kentucky alone, there are provisions which make it *possible* to force a change of masters. But in Louisiana, the master must first be *convicted* of cruel treatment, and, secondly, it is optional with the judge to grant the change of ownership or not. In Kentucky, if the jury shall be satisfied that the slave has been treated cruelly and inhumanly, and so as to

[1] Judge Stroud, *op. cit.* pp. 55—71.
Senator Sumner's Speech, p. 38.
[3] Judge Stroud, *op. cit.* p. 73.

endanger his life or limb, he may be sold to another master. The difficulty, however, of proving cruelty and inhumanity against the master or owner, the testimony of the victim himself, or of any other negro, not being receivable, is so great that this provision of the law must necessarily be almost futile.[1]

But it is often urged that public sentiment at the South is more humane than the law, and does not allow of occurrences which the law itself sanctions. We do not doubt that, in individual instances, the fact is so. Nevertheless, when we consider that the Southern Law-makers have always been chosen from the *élite* of the land, and that the majority of the slave-holders are illiterate and unrefined beings, we are compelled to believe that, in general, the law is more humane than most of the slave-masters, instead of the reverse.

From these and other similar enormities connected with the system of slavery, it results that, even in a purely material view, there is no comparison whatever to be instituted between the condition of the slave and that of the free labourer.

But, "it is written, Man shall not live by bread alone." Nevertheless, the Southern slave has scarce anything else allowed him. The Northern labourer or mechanic is not only able by his own industry to provide for the material wants of himself and his family, but he may, in every considerable town or city, by means of public lectures, by the use of public libraries, by attendance upon night-schools maintained at the public expense or by private liberality, improve himself intellectually and morally to almost any extent. And he is assured that his children will, without expense to himself, receive an education which will fit them for any calling, or for any position in the gift of a free and intelligent people. Nowhere in the world has the industrious labourer who is desirous of improvement, so wide a career as in the Free States of the American Union. Mr. Lincoln, the worthy President of the United States, is an apt illustration of this great and glorious truth—a truth which

1 Judge Stroud, *op. cit.* pp. 93—95. So notoriously cruel and unjust are the decisions of petty tribunals in respect to slaves that, even in South Carolina, a Governor protested to the State Legislature against them as follows: "The administration of our laws in relation to our coloured population, by our courts of magistrates and freeholders, as these courts are at present constituted, calls loudly for reform. Their decisions are rarely in conformity with either justice or humanity."—*Stirling's Letters*, p. 292.

is sneered at only by those whose souls are incapable of appreciating its importance to the millions whom it blesses. The Free States are full of men whom this peculiarity of American institutions has elevated from the position of simple day-labourers and mechanics to that of wealthy, educated and honoured public benefactors, whose children are *the* men of the country. But what future has the Southern slave to look forward to, to cheer and stimulate him in his toil? His brightest anticipation must be that, having lived a slave, like his fathers, he may at death, instead of being buried like a dog, "have a sort of prayers said over him," as the Louisiana overseer told Mr. Russell was sometimes done.[1]

Jefferson, in alluding to the possibility of a slave insurrection, said, "The Almighty has no attribute which can take sides with the slave-holders in such a contest." In view of the multifarious and enormous wickednesses of the system, even as we have only hinted at them in these pages, may we not believe that the Almighty has no attribute which is not in direct hostility to it; and that this war, inaugurated by the South to uphold and perpetuate the institution, must end only with its overthrow?

4. The Free Negroes.

The North is certainly chargeable with injustice in the treatment of the negroes, but to nothing like the degree imputed to it.

In the six New England States the negroes have the same political privileges as the whites; they are citizens; they vote on a par with the whites. In New York and Pennsylvania, and probably in most of the other States, they vote provided they possess a certain property qualification, which, in New York, must be of the value of $25 freehold.

In all the States of the North they are educated at the public expense. In the New England States they frequent the same schools as the whites, no distinction is made; in the other States separate school-rooms are provided. We have seen that

1 See *Ante*, p. 98. For a comparison of the respective conditions of the slaves and free labourers, see Mr. Olmsted's "Journeys and Explorations," vol. ii. chap. vi. The reader will find, too, many details concerning the slaves in the "Report upon the Condition and Management of the Emancipated Negroes in the United States," made to the Secretary of War; this Report was reprinted in the *Daily News*, of London, Sept. 25th and 30th, 1863.

in the Free States a larger proportionate number of coloured youths are instructed at the public expense, than of whites at the South.

As to religious worship, the blacks are as free as the whites. They have their own churches and their own clergymen, and they assemble without restraint or restriction. And there is probably not a community in the Free States where white persons do not contribute, if called upon, to support the religious worship of the negroes.

They have the same rights of person and property as the whites. In the courts of justice they have the same consideration, and their testimony is received with as much respect as that of white men. They inhabit such parts of our towns and cities as they please. In the city of New York they possess property valued at more than $10,000,000; in Philadelphia the value of their property is still greater, their number is larger, and their condition more prosperous even than in New York. Indeed, it is a well-known fact that, in most of our towns and cities, there are scores of black families living in a degree of comfort and of elegance undreamed of by persons of the same station as themselves in any other part of the world. In fact, the prejudice which exists against this class may be fairly said to be much more injurious to the whites, as republicans and Christians, than it is materially prejudicial to the negroes. In proof of this Mr. Olmsted quotes the testimony of several Virginia planters.

The principal fact urged against the people of the Free States as to their treatment of the blacks is, that the latter are not allowed to ride in the same public conveyances as the whites. But this assertion is true only of the cities of Philadelphia and—to a less degree—New York, in both of which there is a considerable number of resident Southern families of wealth and fashion, who have contributed to keep up and increase the prejudice against the negroes. With these insignificant exceptions, the negro travels freely all over the Free States without let or hindrance from his colour.[1]

But how are the free negroes treated at the South?

As was to have been anticipated, the whole spirit of slavery

[1] See Address of Rev. H. W. Beecher, at Manchester, for a statement of the condition of the negroes at the North. *Daily News*, Oct. 12th, 1863.

is hostile to emancipation, not only because this act removes a slave from that toil which is the source of the master's wealth, but because it establishes at the centre of the system a focus of discontent and danger. This aversion to enfranchisement of slaves has grown with the sentiment which upholds slavery. When this institution was regarded as an evil, it was not unusual to give freedom to slaves as a reward for some special act of merit or service, or as an evidence of attachment on the part of the master. But since slavery has come to be regarded as a blessing both to the slave and to the master, laws have been made which render emancipation very rare. In many of the States the slave, when freed, must leave the State under pain of being sold into slavery; in most of the States special permissions must be obtained of the Legislatures or of County Courts, subject to penalties if all the requisitions and restrictions are not complied with on the part both of masters and slaves.

The harsh spirit of the law has been shown repeatedly. Thus, in North Carolina, a free coloured man had accumulated sufficient money to redeem his wife and children from slavery; other children were born to him after the said purchase of the wife's freedom. By the law of the State *all* these were *the father's slaves*, and not free persons as he was. Subsequently the father became involved in debt; his creditors obtained judgments against him, and under these *his wife and children were sold into perpetual slavery.*

In many of the States a slave, who discovers a plot amongst other slaves, or any other crime tending to endanger the public tranquillity or safety, may obtain his freedom by decree of the Legislature.[1]

The free negro, at the South, has no protector or friend; even the law is his enemy; the white man hates and suspects him; the slave despises him. "Poorer than a free nigger," "Worse than a free nigger," are expressions used by slaves when they wish to convey their ideas of a poverty and wretchedness deeper than they themselves even have ever sunk to.

A free negro cannot be a witness in a court of justice, excepting at the trial of another free negro, or slave. He is not allowed to possess or carry fire-arms. If he strike or insult

1 Judge Stroud, *op. cit.* pp. 229–247; *Revue des Deux Mondes*, Dec. 15th, 1860.

a white he is punished by fine, or imprisonment, or both. In some States, if he be the party attacked—and if, in defending himself, he kill the white—he is tried for murder, and not for simple manslaughter.

All assemblages for religious worship must, according to the law, be held in presence of one or more white persons, and only between sunrise and sunset. If a free negro be found in a religious assembly even of white persons, excepting within the hours stated, he is liable to be removed and whipped.

Free negroes, as well as slaves, are allowed to circulate only within certain limits, and with a passport; and if they are caught by the regular patrol, or by any white person, beyond those limits or without their passport, they are liable to arrest and punishment. In Tennessee no free negro is allowed to travel by railway, or other public conveyance, except some white person shall have deposited $1,000 as security. If a free negro leave the State to inhabit some other, and return to the former without permission, he is punished for the first offence by whipping, and for repetition by being sold into perpetual slavery. Any free negro from the North, or from foreign countries, arriving at a Southern port, is immediately arrested and kept in confinement, at the expense of the vessel, so long as the latter shall remain in port.

In the Slave States the law forbids and punishes all attempts to instruct free negroes, either by white persons or negroes, under penalty of imprisonment, fine, or whipping, or all combined.[1]

Until a comparatively recent period free negroes were citizens of North Carolina, and as such claimed and exercised the rights of franchise; but the amended Constitution of that State abrogated to them this privilege.[2] Now they have no right of citizenship in any of the Slave States.

In 1859 the Legislature of Arkansas passed a law of banishment against all free negroes; and all who should be found within the State, at the expiration of one year, were to be sold as slaves to the highest bidder. The Legislature of Missouri enacted a similar law; and also decreed that any free negro from any other State, who should enter Missouri and remain more than twelve hours, should be arrested and sold into

1 *Revue des Deux Mondes*, Dec. 15th, 1860; Judge Stroud, *op. cit.*

2 Livermore, "Historical Research," pp. 6—10.

slavery. The Louisiana Legislature passed a corresponding law. The Legislature of Mississippi granted the free negroes only six months to leave the State on pain of being sold as slaves, and directed that the proceeds of such sales should be paid into the Common School Fund of the State. The Legislature of Georgia enacted that all free negroes, convicted of *idleness* or *immorality*, should be enslaved for one year; and on a repetition of the offence should, if convicted, be sold into perpetual slavery; and that any free negro, convicted and condemned for any offence to the payment of a fine, should, if unable to pay the fine, *be sold* for the benefit of the Treasury.[1]

Petitions[2] signed by many inhabitants of Maryland were presented to the Legislature, praying that the free negroes in that State, 75,000 in number, should be sold as slaves, and distributed amongst the white citizens, on the grounds that "the social and industrial interests of the State, the manifest destiny of the negro race, and the inalienable rights of the whites" demanded this measure; additional reasons assigned were: 1st. "That the free negro does not work, becomes corrupted by idleness, and therefore it is a duty to improve his moral condition by enslaving him." 2nd. That, "by working, the free negro becomes a competitor against the white man, and the preservation of our just prerogative of superiority demands that this immoral competition shall be at once put an end to." These contradictory propositions were not assented to by the Legislature; it did not order the sale of the free negroes, but it did authorize the whites to compel the children of free negroes to labour without the consent of their parents; and it also passed another law authorizing free negroes to sell themselves as slaves.

From these considerations, then, it is manifest that the condition of the free negroes at the North is, beyond comparison, better than at the South. In the former the prejudice against them is but *a prejudice*, local in its operation, and based upon no law; in the latter it is not only an antipathy against their colour, combined with a fear and a suspicion of their influence upon the slaves, but it assumes the form of positive and odious laws. The negroes themselves admit, what indeed is notorious to all observers, that their condition at the North was every year

[1] *Revue des Deux Mondes*, Dec. 15th, 1860.

[2] Ibid.

improving, even before the war.[1] Since this great crisis the prejudice against them has been fast disappearing, in consequence partly of the good conduct and bravery of those of them who have enlisted into the army, and partly because the nation has awakened to a consciousness of its wrong-doing towards them.[2] Colour, as a badge and symbol of inferiority and servitude, is disappearing with slavery, and we do not doubt that soon the negro will willingly be admitted to all the privileges, rights, and immunities of citizenship, on the broadest basis of equality with the whites. Every fact shows that the negro has participated in, and progressed with, the general advancement of society in the Free States. This must necessarily continue more unrestrictedly than before the war. But at the South, so long as slavery endures, the condition of the free blacks must inevitably grow worse and worse.

1 Stirling's "Letters."

2 It is almost impossible to keep pace with the progress being made in this direction. Less than a year ago, Sella Martin, a coloured preacher in New York, wrote as follows to the *Star*, of June 4th, 1863 : "There are now coloured men employed by the United States Government as officers in the custom-houses of New York and Boston. Coloured men have been commissioned as surgeons in the army ; coloured soldiers are received on an equality with white soldiers ; and there is at this moment presiding over one of the wealthiest Presbyteries of the city of Brooklyn, a coloured man who is not yet forty years of age." Since that time more than 50,000 coloured men have been enlisted into the army, and several thousands into the naval service, in which they mess with white sailors. Some of the best white officers in the service have been eager to obtain command in negro regiments ; negro soldiers are placed upon a perfect equality with white, as regards pay and rations ; and in case of levying of troops by conscription, they are to be placed on the same footing. Negro regiments marching through our cities now are received as enthusiastically as white troops, and banners and colours are presented to them by the fairest in the land. And the negro soldiers are as brave and as well disciplined under the hottest fire as any in the army. The prejudice against the blacks at the North has been chiefly confined to the labouring population of our cities, and especially to the foreigners, with whom the negroes come into competition as labourers. But the supply of labour has become so unequal to the demand, in consequence of the ravages of the war, that, for some years, at least, the whites will scarcely feel this competition. Hence an additional source of improvement in the condition of the blacks.

VII.

COMPARATIVE PROGRESS AND RESOURCES OF NORTH AND SOUTH.

A FEW statistics will show conclusively how slavery, by limiting the kind and quality of labour, and by preventing the due development of the resources of the Slave States, has impeded their progress.

The South boasts of being an agricultural country, and to agriculture has been devoted almost exclusively the capital and energy of the people. Yet, notwithstanding this concentration of forces they have been far excelled by their Northern brethren even in this very field of their choice.

In 1850, the value of the agricultural products of the Slave States, including cotton, rice, tobacco, and sugar, was estimated at $461,129,746, that of the animals slaughtered for food, $54,395,415,—total $515,525,161; of the free States, agricultural products, $566,130,832, animals slaughtered, $61,157,617 —total $627,288,449; difference in favour of the Free States, $112,163,288.

The South points with triumph to her cotton-crop, as being the great regulator of the foreign exchange for the United States. In fact, it was the possession of this great staple of which the Slave States held almost the monopoly, and the possession of which was of such momentous importance to Europe, and especially to England, which the Southern leaders believed would secure the success of their rebellion, inasmuch as it would insure European interference in their behalf. This was avowed by the *Southern Quarterly Review*, at the outbreak of the war. But the noble and intelligent patience and fortitude of the British people, combined with the unexpected resources and patriotism of the Northern States, have shown the comparative insignificance of cotton:

In 1850 the value of the Indian corn crop was		£59,207,110
„ „	Wheat „	20,097,188
„ „	Cotton „	19,720,744

In 1860, value of the Indian corn crop of the United States, £99,654,204

„ „	Wheat „	51,355,014
„ „	Hay „	42,849,246
„ „	Cotton „	33,267,692
„ „	Oats „	32,526,444

In 1862, the second year of the war, the exports from the single port of New York, when not a bale of cotton left the harbour, amounted in value to 1,000,000*l.* more than the entire exports of all the slave-holding States in 1859, when their cotton-crop alone was estimated at 40,000,000*l.*[1] Such is the recuperative energy and capacity of a free people, which has enabled the Government, thus far, to carry the country through this tremendous struggle, and which, we believe, will bring it to a triumphant conclusion.

The aggregate value of the farms, the implements and machinery used for agricultural purposes, together with the live stock, was, for the Free States $2,415,265,890; for the Slave States $1,436,709,923; estimating the slaves as worth $400 each, their aggregate value was $1,280,121,600, making the entire capital invested in the Slave States in agriculture (assuming that all the slaves are so employed, which is not strictly correct), $2,716,831,523. Thus we find that although the capital invested in this way at the South was $301,565,633 greater than at the North, the revenue derived from the same in the former was $112,163,288 less than in the latter section. This shows conclusively that, in spite of superior fertility of soil and of a milder climate, which, in many ways, makes agricultural operations less expensive, slave labour is far inferior to free labour.

The same important truth is evident if we compare the productiveness of the two sections with respect to particular crops. In 1850, the average yield of *Wheat* was 12 bushels per acre in the Free States, against 9 in the Slave States; of *Oats*, 27 bushels against 9; of *Rye*, 18 bushels against 11; of *Indian Corn*, 31

[1] Bigelow, "Les Etats-Unis en 1863."

bushels against 20 ; of *Potatoes,* 125 bushels against 113. Massachusetts, with a cold and rocky soil, produced 16 bushels of wheat per acre, Virginia only 7; Pennsylvania 15, Georgia 5. Iowa yielded 36 bushels of oats per acre, Mississippi 12; Rhode Island 30, North Carolina 10. Ohio returned 25 bushels of rye per acre, Kentucky 11; Vermont 20, Tennessee 7. Connecticut produced 40 bushels of Indian corn per acre, Texas, with its virgin soil, 20; New Jersey 33, South Carolina 11. New Hampshire yielded 220 bushels of potatoes per acre, Maryland 75 ; Michigan 140, Alabama 60.[1]

In 1849-50, the comparative productiveness of Ohio, a Free State, admitted into the Union only in 1802, and of Virginia, a Slave State, colonised in 1607, was as follows, in two chief articles of production :—Ohio, possessing 9,851,493 acres of improved land in farms, yielded, with other products, 59,078,695 bushels of Indian corn, and 10,454,449 pounds of tobacco, valued in total at $36,769,815 ; Virginia, possessing 10,360,135 acres of improved land in farms, yielded, with other products, but more limited than Ohio, 35,254,319 bushels of Indian corn, and 56,803,227 pounds of tobacco, of the aggregate value of $25,481,358, leaving a surplus, in favour of Ohio, of $11,288,457 from these two products alone. The average yield in Ohio was 36 bushels of Indian corn, and 730 pounds of tobacco per acre; in Virginia, 18 bushels of the former, and 630 pounds of the latter.

A similar disparity exists in the average value of land. In the Free States, in 1850, the average value per acre was $10·47, in the Slave States, $3·04. In 1855 the value per acre was $14·72 against 4·59. Comparing particular States, the difference becomes still more striking. In 1854, 17,289,359 acres of land were assessed in South Carolina, the model Slave State, as her friends delight to call her, at the average value of $1·30 per acre; in New Jersey, 5,324,800 acres were valued at $28·76 per acre. In 1856, in New York, 30,080,000 acres were assessed at the average value of $36·97 per acre; in North Carolina, 32,450,560 acres were valued at $3·06 per acre. In Virginia, the average value of land was $8·00 per acre; in Pennsylvania, $25·00 per acre.

From these comparative statements, it is quite evident that the opinion long entertained by many of the most thoughtful and

[1] Helper, *op. cit.* 65.

intelligent men at the South is correct, viz. that emancipation will eventually more than compensate the capital invested in the slaves, by the enhanced value of the land, and by the increased productiveness of the soil, owing to a better system of agriculture which it would speedily induce.[1]

If we examine into the relative increase of population, and into the comparative wealth, of the two sections, we are still struck with the depressing and baneful effect of slavery; for the Slave States presented, as we have seen, very great natural advantages as inducements to settlers.

In 1790, the Free States comprised 1,968,455 inhabitants, the Slave States, 1,961,372—a difference in favour of the former of 7,083. In 1850, the population of the latter, augmented by the annexation of three foreign territories—Louisiana, Florida, and Texas—had increased to 9,612,769; while that of the Free States, without any such annexations, had risen to 13,238,670 ; in other words, the difference in population had increased from 7,083, in 1790, to 4,625,901 in 1850. In the Slave States the average density of population was 11·28 per square mile, in the Free States 21·93.

The aggregate value of the real and personal property in the Free States, in 1850, was $4,153,575,629 ; of the Slave States, including the slaves, $2,982,204,599.[2] The population of the six original slave-holding States was, at the time of the adoption of the Constitution, greater by more than a hundred thousand than that of the seven original free States, and the wealth of the former was much greater than that of the latter. But in 1850 the population of the former was only 4,591,645, while that of the latter was 7,729,562; the total value of the real and personal

[1] Mr. Olmsted, Mr. Stirling, and others, have taken pains to ascertain the comparative cost of labour in the two sections of our country, and they find that free labour is not only cheaper, in view of the actual wages paid, but infinitely more so when the amount and excellence of the work done by slaves and free labourers are considered, the loss of labour produced by age, infirmities and sickness of slaves, &c. &c. Now, as the author of the "Boston Trade Report" remarks, could the South have but understood that the slaves would have done more and better work if they had been paid, in the form of wages, the interest upon the capital invested in them as *chattels;* and if it had placed this capital in railways, canals, farm-improvements, commercial and manufacturing towns, and the thousand interest-paying securities represented in the North, the prosperity of the Slave States could scarcely be imagined.

[2] *National Almanac* for 1863, p. 147.

property in the former was $1,521,464,882, including the slaves, while that of the Free States was $2,916,007,231.[1]

A similar contrast is presented if we compare the manufacturing and every other department of industry, in the two sections, although the slave-holding States possess greater natural advantages, both for manufacturing and commercial purposes.

Manufactures, 1860.	Free States.	Slave States.
No. of establishments	100,346	27,954
Capital invested	$849,025,000	$201,975,000
Raw material used	$853,935,000	$158,065,000
No. of persons employed	1,181,485	203,515
Value of annual product [2]	$1,616,812,000	$283,188,000

In 1855, the import and export trade of the Free States amounted to $404,368,503, of the Slave States to $132,067,216. The exports of the former were valued at $167,520, 693, of the latter, including cotton, at $132,007,216. The imports of the Free States were estimated at $236,847,810, of the Slave States at $24,586,528. The foreign commerce of New York alone was more than twice as great as that of all the Slave States combined.[3]

In 1854 there were 13,105 miles of railways, and 3,682 miles of canals in operation in the Free States; 4,212 miles of railways and 1,116 miles of canals in operation in the Slave States.[4]

Thus we see how, under the influence and exigencies of their inferior labour system, the Slave States have been compelled to neglect and waste their immense natural resources and advantages.

The comparative value of freedom and slavery, as the basis of "national life," is strikingly shown if we contrast the two States which are models of these two systems respectively, Massachusetts and South Carolina. In the former we have a pure democracy, in the latter an aristocracy (such as it is), based upon slavery.

The population of Massachusetts in 1790, was 378,717, of which none were slaves; South Carolina had 357,567 inhabitants,

[1] *National Almanac*, pp. 307, 328.
[2] Ibid. p. 323.
[3] Senator Sumner's "Speech on the Barbarism of Slavery," p. 24.
[4] Ibid.

of whom 107,694 were slaves. But in 1860 the population of Massachusetts had augmented to 1,231,066, that of South Carolina to 703,708, of which 402,406 were slaves. In other words, Massachusetts had gained, during seventy years, a population of 852,349 free men, South Carolina only 51,429. The former State has a density of population of 157·82 per square mile, the latter of 23·29—so greatly does slavery interfere with this important element of national prosperity.

In climate and natural fertility of soil, these two States are the antipodes of each other. In point of comparative salubrity, also, they differ materially: the mortality from disease having been in 1860, as 1 to 60·36 of the population in Massachusetts, and as 1 to 77·22 in Carolina.

In 1760, the imports into Charleston were valued at $2,662,000, considerably more than the imports of Boston. But in 1860-61, the imports of Carolina had fallen to $806,480, those of Massachusetts had augmented to $45,399,844. The exports from Carolina, in 1860–61 were valued at $5,455,581, including cotton, rice and everything else; the exports from Massachusetts, at $16,572,736.

The various manufacturing establishments, mines, &c. &c., of Massachusetts, in 1860 yielded a revenue of $266,001,800, and furnished employment to 217,100 persons; those of Carolina yielded $7,860,594, and employed 6,800 persons. In addition the product of the fisheries, in which Massachusetts is largely interested, was estimated at more than $3,000,000. Unfortunately, the Census returns do not furnish data for the annual revenue derived by individuals from commerce, in which Massachusetts far exceeds Carolina.

Agricultural Statistics, 1860.	Massachusetts.	South Carolina.
Area in acres	4,992,000	18,805,400
No. of acres in cultivated farms	2,155,512	4,572,060
,, ,, non-cultivated farms	1,183,212	11,623,860
Value of farms, per acre	$36·88	$8·62
,, agricultural implements, &c.	$ 3,894,998	$ 6,151,657
,, live-stock	13,137,748	23,932,465
,, animals slaughtered	2,515,045	6,072,822
,, agricultural products	15,151,991	38,821,722

If we analyse these figures we shall get some important results:—

Agricultural Statistics, 1860.	Massachusetts.	South Carolina.
Value of agricultural implements, &c. per acre	$1·16	$ ·37
,, live-stock per acre	3·93	1·47
,, animals slaughtered, per acre . .	·87	·37
,, agricultural products, ,, . .	4·53	2·39

From this table it results that South Carolina, although pre-eminently an agricultural country, and possessing an immense annual crop of the finest cotton grown anywhere, is far surpassed by Massachusetts even in respect to agriculture.

Dividing the total annual revenue acquired by the people of Massachusetts—exclusive of that derived from commerce and trade, from scientific, literary and professional pursuits, from personal property and real estate, &c. &c., in all of which the inhabitants of Massachusetts are infinitely more interested than those of Carolina—by the total population, we find that each inhabitant gained, on an average, $233·38, in 1860. Making the same calculation for Carolina, each of her inhabitants gained but $76·15.

The aggregate value of the real and personal property in Massachusetts was $815,237,433; in Carolina $544,138,754, including slaves.

There were in 1860, 1,195 miles of railway in operation in Massachusetts, against 570 miles in Carolina.

Educational Statistics, &c. 1860-62.	Massachusetts.	South Carolina.
No. of persons from five to twenty years old	283,000	114,280
No. of these at the public schools	220,030	19,132
Annual expense of the public schools . .	$1,610,823	$196,300
No. of ignorant native whites	1,055	15,580
No. of ignorant foreign ,, ...	26,484	104
No. of universities, colleges, professional and scientific schools, &c.	15	10
No. of students attending these	2,000	501
No. of academies and private schools . .	709	Not given.
No. of students attending these	19,825	,, ,,
No. of public libraries (1850)	1,462	26
No. of volumes contained in these . . .	684,015	107,472
No. of journals, periodicals, &c. published .	202	46
Annual circulation of these	64,820,564	7,145,930

Of course, no count is made of the black population of Carolina, in which, according to the above table, $\frac{1}{17}$th of the white population can neither read nor write, while in Massachusetts only $\frac{1}{100}$ of the population is thus ignorant. It is estimated that the aggregate sum paid in Massachusetts for educational purposes, in maintaining the public schools, and in defraying the expenses of private education, amounted in 1862 to $3,100,000 (*National Almanac*, p. 374). We have not enumerated the institutions for the education of the blind, of the deaf and dumb, of idiotic persons, nor the educational establishments connected with the prisons and various Reformatory Institutions of Massachusetts. Neither have we referred to the many Institutions of public lectureships in every large town of the State, nor to the numerous private means set on foot for the moral and intellectual training of the people.

The value of the religious edifices in Massachusetts, in 1850, was $10,504,888, in Carolina $2,181,476. In the former, $263,545 were contributed to the various religious publication societies, in the latter, $16,104; to the Society for Domestic Missions $47,607 in Massachusetts, but *nothing* in Carolina.

The reader who is curious concerning these comparisons between the Free and Slave-holding States will find many such in the able "Letters" of the Hon. R. J. Walker, on American Finances and Resources—London, 1863-4; Ridgway, 169 Piccadilly. For our statistics, we refer to the *National Almanac* and the other authorities already cited.

If we compare the condition of the States which have remained true to the Union with that of the States composing the Confederacy, we shall see the great material loss which the latter have suffered in consequence of the refusal of a portion of the Slave States to secede with them. And we shall likewise see the comparative resources of the two sections now at war.

In 1860, the value of the agricultural products of the loyal States was estimated at $1,065,456,252, of the Confederate States at $516,546,140, leaving a balance in favour of the former of $548,910,112.

Manufactures, 1860.	Loyal States.	Confederacy.
No. of establishments	110,274	18,026
Capital invested	$949,335,000	$100,665,000
Raw material consumed	$929,391,000	$82,609,000
No. of persons employed	1,274,890	110,110
Value of annual products	$1,754,650,000	$145,350,000

L

Banking Statistics, 1860.	Loyal States.	Confederacy.
Capital of Banks	$332,241,336	$113,124,421
Specie	56,333,952	27,260,585
Funds equivalent to specie	18,203,398	1,138,123
Circulation	147,643,192	59,459,285
Loans and discounts	544,991,037	142,954,543
Deposits	210,922,817	42,879,112

In 1860, there were in operation in the loyal States 21,846.77 miles of railway, built at a cost of $917,134,732, and 4,607 miles of canals. In the Confederate States, 8,946.90 miles of railway, built at a cost of $237,426,097, and 566 miles of canals.

The shipping owned in the loyal States, in 1860, amounted to 4,750,179 tons; in the Confederate States, 351,797 tons. The exports from the former were valued at $178,604,334; from the latter at $178,340,776; the imports of the former at $315,522,166, of the latter at $23,230,831.

Property, &c. 1860.[1]	Loyal States.	Confederacy.
Acres of improved land in farms	105,015,314	57,092,633
Cash value of farms	$4,777,933,587	$1,870,938,920
Value of farming implements, &c. . . .	163,013,553	83,993,793
,, live-stock	716,527,942	390,962,274
,, animals slaughtered	131,389,352	81,542,301
,, real estate and personal property, including slaves (at $500)	10,900,758,009	5,202,166,167[2]

In connexion with this statement of the comparative industry and resources of the two sections, the question of their respective debts, and of their ability to support these charges, naturally presents itself.

As to the Confederate States, we know that their natural resources are immense; but we know, also, that these never can be developed under slave labour, which it is the avowed aim and intention of these States to perpetuate. We know likewise that most of the States have positively refused to guarantee, individually, the Confederate Debt. By a report published in the

[1] For statistics we have referred to the *National Almanac*, 1863; Helper's Book; Ellison's "Slavery and Secession in America;" Bigelow, "LesEtats-Unis en 1863."

[2] The slaves are both producers and consumers; and, consequently, though called *property*, they do not economically belong to that category. If we subtract this element, we shall leave to the Confederacy only $3,467,105,667 of property.

Richmond Examiner, Dec. 1863, the debt of the Confederacy was stated to be $1,210,441,965, or more than $200 for each white inhabitant of the Confederate States. Now, the National Debt of Great Britain, which the British people, with all their wealth, industry, energy, and resources, would be very unwilling to see increased, was in the ratio of $132·61 to each inhabitant of the United Kingdom in 1861, a sum very much less than that which presses upon the Southern people, whose resources are vastly less and more limited. In fact, the hopelessness of attempting to sustain such a debt has been virtually proclaimed by the Confederate Congress itself, in a manner which has called forth earnest protests from leading Southern journals, and from such prominent men as the Governor of Georgia, who, in his recent message to the Legislature of that State, criticises the late financial measures of the Congress as follows: "The compulsory funding of seven hundred millions of dollars in forty days, at a less rate of interest than that pledged on full notes, resembles repudiation and bad faith."[1]

The effects which the secession of the Confederate States has produced upon the general prosperity of the rest of the Union are among the most astounding results of the war. It was predicted at the South that, as a consequence of the crisis, the prosperity of the North, which was fancied to be based upon its connexion with the South, would be paralysed. The result has been far otherwise.

Secession has diminished the expenditures of the Post-Office Department of the United States by nearly $5,000,000. The value of the mechanical and manufactured products of the loyal States has increased $330,227,359 in 1863, as compared with 1860; the value of their domestic exports has increased $73,476,941 in 1862, as compared with 1860; the revenue from Customs has augmented from $39,582,125, for the year ending June 30, 1861, to $93,934,436 (actual and estimated) for the year 1864. In all departments of business, increased activity and prosperity are manifest. Thus, in Philadelphia, during the first four months of 1860 there were 636 buildings in process of erection, against 911 during the corresponding months of 1863. The book-trade is in a more flourishing condition now than it ever was before secession, notwithstanding an increase of at least

[1] *Daily News*, March 31st, 1864.

25 per cent. in the expenses of book-making; and the sales are for cash, instead of on long credits, as was the trade with the South before the war. The Reports of the Savings' Banks in the five principal cotton-manufacturing towns of Massachusetts, which were imagined to be dependent on the South, show that the number of depositors had increased 2,687, and the amount of deposits $1,162,264, in 1862, as compared with 1860. The Bank Commissioners of Massachusetts report, that there has been an increase of 23,842 depositors, and of $5,618,235 deposits in the Savings' Banks, in 1862–3, as compared with 1859–60.

The Slave States, according to Vice-President Stephens, contributed less than one-fourth to the ordinary revenues of the Government. The proportion of taxes to be assessed upon the Confederate States, under the Tax Law of 1861, was but a trifle more than one-fifth of those levied upon the loyal States, although three-fifths of the slaves were rated in addition to the white inhabitants. So much for the loss from secession.

As to the ability of the loyal States alone to support the debt of the United States, we have the benefit of historical lights, as well as the knowledge of our own resources, to guide us to a conclusion.

On the 29th January, 1864, the Official Report of the United States Debt fixed the total amount at $1,446,371,507, of which $756,717,809 bore interest. The debt is, of course, daily increasing, and must increase so long as the war shall continue. But taking its present amount as a basis for present calculation, and comparing it with the resources of the loyal States only, we arrive at the following results; comparing together the debts of England, France, and the United States in 1816, and of the loyal States, in 1864:

	Public Debt.	Debt per Caput.	Per cent. ratio of debt to Property.	Value of Real and Personal Property.	Value of Annual Products.	Per cent. ratio of Debt to Annual Products.
Great Britain 1816	$4,299,824,588	$222·79	$41·14	$10,450,000,000	——	——
,, 1861	3,890,155,911	132·61	12.34	31,512,000,000	——	——
France. . . 1863	2,304,000,000	61·79	9·47	——	——	——
United States 1791	75,463,476	18·55	10·06	750,000,000	——	——
,, 1816	127,334,933	14·67	7·07	1,800,000,000	$ 454,500,000	25¼
Loyal States. 1864	1,446,371,507	57·85	9·95	14,533,980,653	3,822,436,911	37·8

The population of the loyal States in 1864 is at least 25,000,000. The total property of their population increased in value, from 1850 to 1860, 126½ per cent.; in the table we have estimated the increase in value from 1860 to 1864 at only 33⅓ per cent. so as to be within bounds. The annual value of those products of industry alone which the Census notices, was, for 1860, 26·3 per cent. of the valuation of the property; we shall certainly be considered as warranted to estimate the products of 1863–4 upon the same per-centage, as we have done in the above table. But we will remark that the Census return gives a very incomplete representation of the annual industrial products of the country. The Census takes no note of the agricultural products and domestic manufactures of our farmers consumed by their families and their *employés,* who form almost three-fourths of our total population; again, the vast total of mechanical products which individually fall below the value of $500 per annum is omitted; nor is any notice taken of the labour employed in clearing and improving lands, in building and repairing railways, canals, houses, manufactories, vessels, nor of the gains of domestic and foreign trade and commerce, &c. &c. It is estimated that nearly one-half of the annual yield of the country is thus omitted from the Census returns.

From a comparison of the debt and resources of the loyal States in 1864 with those of the United States in 1816, we certainly have nothing to fear. The United States Debt of 1816 was all paid, capital and interest, in the course of eighteen years, and three years afterwards there was a surplus in the Treasury of $36,000,000. In two most important respects we have great advantages for the payment of our debt, as compared with our fathers. Our recently-established banking system, besides giving us an uniform currency for the whole country, and immediately interesting the whole population in the financial credit of the Government, saves, by the use of United States notes, many millions annually to the Government, and greatly reduces the interest on the debt. Another marked advantage which we possess, not only over our fathers, but also over Great Britain during the years when the larger portion of her debt was accumulated, consists in the fact that, with small exceptions, the money which we are expending is being expended at home, and has been all raised amongst our own people, instead of having been borrowed abroad, as was the case with the United States Government loans of 1776–1816, and spent abroad in paying armies fighting in foreign lands and in subsidizing foreign allies, as was the case with the large proportion of British expenditures for many years.

The confidence of the people in the loyal States in the financial stability of the Government, and in the ability of the country to support the weight of an immense debt, is shown in the facility with which money has been obtained, and the rates of interest paid. During the last quarter of Mr. Buchanan's Administration a loan was negotiated at 11 per cent. interest; in April, May, and July, of 1861, the present Secretary of the Treasury sold his first loans at an average discount of 10.91 per cent. at 6 per cent. interest; later in the same year a larger loan was negotiated *at par,* at $7\frac{3}{10}$ per cent. interest; no other loans have been sold below par. The United States loans of 1799 and 1800 were sold at a discount of 17.29 per cent.; those of 1813 at 12 and 11·75 per cent.; those of March, 1814, at 19·86 per cent. discount; and the total discounted loans from 1799 to 4th March, 1861, were sold at an average discount of 12·55 per cent.

The normal prices of the British 3 per cents. being 93, and standing always above 89 from 1730 to 1745, they fell during the Scotch Rebellion of 1745 to 76; at the close of the American War to 54; in 1797 to $47\frac{3}{8}$; and during the Crimean War to $85\frac{1}{8}$. On the other hand, the United States 6 per Cent. Twenty Year Coupon Bonds stood at 89–92 in September, 1861; at 98 in April, 1862; at $107\frac{1}{4}$ in June, 1862; at 100–104 between July and December; at 99–$106\frac{1}{2}$ from January to April, 1863; and at $112\frac{1}{2}$ on March 26th, 1864.

We are told that the currency is enormously "inflated," and that "the bubble" must collapse and scatter immense ruin over the country. We can hardly expect to escape considerable financial embarrassment and trouble. But, nevertheless, the prospect is less dismal than some would have it. The United States Currency Notes, which represent a large portion of the Public Debt, and which are used by the Treasury as a medium of payment in defraying the enormous war expenditures of the country, amounted on the 29th January, 1864, to $689,653,698, or $27.58 per loyal inhabitant, no specie being circulated. In 1815 the paper circulation of Great Britain amounted to

$706,000,000, or $37.15 per head of the population; while her wealth at that time was *four thousand millions of dollars* less than that of the loyal States of America in 1864. Yet the paper-money of England, three years after its lowest depreciation and after twenty years' suspension of specie payments, was "as good as gold." From 1852 to 1859 the average bank-note circulation of the loyal States was $146,000,000, or $9.06 per head of the population and this in specie-paying times. In May, 1863, the bank-note circulation of the loyal States amounted to $168,400,000 or $7 per head of their population; and it had become more secure and is daily improving in this respect by being based (with reference to those banks which adopt the system sanctioned by Congress in 1863), not only upon private capital, but also upon adequate deposits, with the Government, of United States Stocks. Thus, we see that the proportional amount of bank-paper to the population has really diminished, and that its character has improved. And as to the Treasury paper, in May, 1863, the Secretary of the Treasury was able *to fund it at the rate of two millions of dollars per diem.*

The payment in gold of the interest on that portion of the public debt which is payable in gold, is secured upon the Customs receipts, which must be paid in specie. These receipts are "set apart" for the specific objects of paying the gold-bearing interest of the debt, and of purchasing for a sinking fund so much of the principal of the public debt as shall amount in gold, within each fiscal year, to 1 per cent. of the whole debt. This source is unfailing, and, excepting for the contingency of a foreign war with some great naval Power, must increase in fertility with the increase of the population and the general development of the country.

The great resources upon which we rely for our ability to sustain any amount of indebtedness which is likely to come upon us are—the settlement and development of new lands, by an increasing population; the products of our mines of precious metals; and the continued progress of the old States.

In the region of the public lands belonging to the Government, the private property of the inhabitants increased, from 1850 to 1860, from $452,000,000 to $2,512,000,000, and the population from 2,613,000 to 6,027,000, or 130 per cent. The Government still possesses 964,901,625 acres of these lands undisposed of. It is not presumptuous to anticipate that, under the operation of the Homestead law, and of the ordinary causes which have been in operation for some years, a continued development in resources and population will occur.

Again, the enormous wealth locked up in the auriferous region of the United States, which comprises seventeen degrees of latitude and almost as many of longitude, forming an area of more than a million of square miles, cannot be easily over-estimated. It embraces, besides its great variety of mineral treasures, a vast expanse of territory admirably adapted to agricultural purposes. To give access to this region, and to develope its capabilities, a railway, which will connect the valley of the Mississippi with the Pacific, is now in process of construction.

And in the meantime the old States have, within the last ten years, more than doubled the capital of their wealth, and added $41\frac{1}{2}$ per cent. to their free population; each Census shows a similar progress.[1]

[1] For our facts and reasoning concerning the financial condition and prospects of the country, we are indebted to an admirable pamphlet on the "Debt and Resources of the United States," by Dr. William Elder, of the Treasury Department: Philadelphia, 1863.

CONCLUSION.

We have finished the task which we had allotted to ourselves. We have shown what are the sentiments and policy of the Southern people on the question of slavery, and that these have been gradually becoming more and more determined in favour of that system. We have traced their schemes for acquiring new slave territory at home and abroad, and for re-establishing the African slave-trade; and we have shown that the very men who have been the most prominent leaders in the secession movement of the Confederacy, are they who have most favoured slavery extension. We have demonstrated the immense progress which the Free States have made as compared with the South, and that the only primary cause of the inferiority of the latter is this very institution, which Southern independence was designed to perpetuate.

We believe we have proved that the States composing the Southern Confederacy possessed no *right of secession* from the Union to which they and their inhabitants owed allegiance, and that they had never been subjected to any oppression which would justify rebellion. We have shown beyond question that the great first cause of the rebellion was the desire and determination of the Southern leaders to uphold and perpetuate an institution which they saw was remotely, though surely, endangered by the Union, under the recently inaugurated supremacy of Northern sentiment. For the first time in the history of the world, as the Southern Vice-President boasted, the attempt is being made by a professedly Christian people, aided by their religious teachers, to establish the most odious conceivable despotism, by founding a civil Government based avowedly upon negro slavery.

The distinctive social and political characteristics of the two parties arrayed against each other in the war thus inaugurated, are so clearly marked, that there can be no hesitation as to the side on which right and wrong respectively predominates. On one side is a well-ordered Government, "ordained and established to promote the *general* welfare, and to secure the blessings of *liberty* to ourselves and our posterity." These results it has, according to the general testimony of all mankind, accomplished for its white subjects; and it has failed in its original object of securing these blessings to all, without distinction of colour, only because this object has been thwarted and falsified by the party now in open arms against it. On the other side, the founders of the new Confederacy avow that it is based upon slavery as its corner-stone; and its *mission*, as declared by its clerical expounders, is "to extend and perpetuate slavery." On one side, we have seen that the diffusion of education, religious and secular, is regarded as a prominent obligation both of Governments and people, and that this duty has been nobly attended to. On the other side, we find it taught that "the policy which discourages the farther extension of knowledge amongst the poor whites and the blacks is necessary," and that "a system of common-school education is impossible." On one side, labour is honoured, and industry enabled to surround itself with all those means and appliances which conduce to prosperity and happiness. On the other side, labour is considered as a disgrace, and the poor of the land, the millions, "are condemned to hopeless ignorance, poverty, and crime." On one side, freedom of thought, freedom of speech, freedom of the press, are natural and necessary results of political institutions and public sentiment. On the other side, "Slavery is omnipresent, thought is not free." In short, on the side of the Free States we find accomplished, or being accomplished, all those great objects after which European nations have been striving ever since the middle ages; and within the Southern Confederacy we see congregated most of the social and political evils which Europe has been struggling to throw off, and negro slavery in addition.

Of all people on the face of the globe the English, one would have had a right *à priori* to suppose, would have been the last to hesitate as to which was the side of right and justice and duty in this matter. For the greater part of the present century, opposition to African slavery has been a proud boast of the English Government and people. One may even say, without wish or intention to offend, that the legislation of the British Government on this question has been *the only unselfish* policy which that Government has ever pursued on any question; for it had for its object the suppression of the wrongs and the alleviation of the miseries of a race not English, and not inhabiting the United Kingdom. One of the chief faults which England has charged, and justly, against the United States, has been the support given by the latter to this odious institution. Both the Government and the people of England have unceasingly protested to the Government and the people of the United States against this support, as a gross violation of human rights and of the principles of Christianity. A few years ago, an Address, splendidly illuminated on vellum, and signed by more than half a million of British women, not only of England but of her dependencies, was presented to the women of America. Amongst the signers were most of the noble ladies of England, including the wives of probably all the ministers of the Crown. These ladies acknowledged, "with grief and shame," the share which England had borne in fastening slavery upon America; but, said they, "it is because we so deeply feel and so unfeignedly avow our own complicity, that we now venture to implore your aid to wipe away our common crime and our common dishonour."

The merits of the great chronic controversy between the North and South, which finally, upon the election of Mr. Lincoln to the Presidency, culminated in the present war, were fully understood and recognised in England. The extracts[1] which we have already given from "the leading journal of England," prove that this great organ and guide of public sentiment apprehended the issues involved as clearly as any American could have done. And they show also that the *Times*, knowing what English principles and policy had been on this subject, did not doubt, then, that England would judge and act as became that great nation which so loudly proclaims her enlightened Christian, liberal, and anti-slavery principles. The people of the Northern States did unquestionably entertain the same belief. They did not expect or desire English aid in suppressing this slave-holders' rebellion. But they did believe that a hearty British cheer would roll over the Atlantic, bidding them God-speed; they did believe that Christian, anti-slavery England would hold aloft the emblem of our common faith, as it appeared of old to Constantine, and bid them fight the good fight.

But, unhappily, Governments are more frequently guided in

[1] See *ante*, p. 61.

their dealings with each other by interest than by principles of morality and justice. Jealousy of a growing rival, aversion to democratic success, or some other petty motive which Englishmen feel, but do not care always to avow, have led the ruling classes of England—and, to a certain extent, the English Government—to adopt a line of policy towards the belligerents which has justly thrown suspicion upon the sincerity of English professions concerning slavery. Even the religious bodies of Great Britain have, in general, formed no exception to this rule. The British branch of the Evangelical Alliance refused, a year ago, to unite with its French colleagues in an expression of satisfaction at the progress made in the United States towards abolition. The Free Church of Scotland has shown itself particularly hostile to us, nothwithstanding its former repeated denunciations of the churches in America for their support or toleration of slavery. When words of encouragement would have been a slight, yet an acceptable, return for the substantial aid [1] it had received from our churches and people in its own hour of want and weakness, all its favour has been given to the South. Its chief organ has declared, "We solemnly rejoice in the dismemberment of the Union." Even the liberal *Edinburgh Review* has proclaimed, that "The North has no more right to force its policy upon the South, than the South has to infect the North with the taint of slavery;" this is said of a country whose constitution, established by the people, ordains that the majority, properly declared, shall govern. The British press, with a few notable examples to the contrary, has, in criticising the characters and policy of the leading men of the North, from the President downwards, employed language, under the cowardly shield of an incognito, which would have disgraced the *New York Herald* in its worst days. Similar language has been used by very many public speakers both in and out of Parliament. An aspirant to a seat in the House of Commons—a man whose name is more hopeful than his political principles, and who has rivalled *Blackwood's Magazine* in vulgar abuse of

[1] We well remember to have heard that, when the delegates sent to the United States to solicit alms and aid in behalf of the infant Free Church of Scotland reported that, in addition to the large sums obtained at the North, they had also received contributions from the South, placards were posted upon the walls in Edinburgh, demanding that the money obtained from slave-holders should be returned. In those days, less than twenty years ago, opposition to slavery seems to have been *a principle* in Scotland.

the President of the United States—declared, scarce a year ago, in a speech at Maidstone, that "the cause of the Southern Federation is the cause of freedom, is the cause of English feeling, is the cause of constitutional Government all over the world." With a few distinguished exceptions,

"rari nantes in gurgite vasto,"

those members of Parliament who have expressed their sentiments, have avowed themselves warm partizans of the South. Alone, of all the ministry, the Foreign Secretary—whose name and life-long efforts in behalf of political liberty and progress entitle him to be the standard-bearer of England against this latest and most repulsive attempt at despotism—has borne, in the legislative halls of his country, a noble testimony in favour of principle against selfishness.[1] In short, the only country on the face of the globe, out of America, from which the "Slave Republic" has met with encouragement and direct material aid, is that very country whence it had the least apparent right to hope for either—Great Britain, from British merchants, shippers, ship-builders and manufacturers, the British press, the British aristocracy, the British churches. Thus, the anti-slavery sentiment of Great Britain, which had hitherto been regarded abroad as a great and solid fact upon which all the world might lean, has come to seem, after all, to be of "such stuff as dreams are made of"; it has almost vanished before the more subtle and more deeply-rooted passion of jealous hostility against the United States. The mass of the British people, which is considered unworthy or incompetent to share in the legislation of the country, has manifested, during all this American contest, an appreciation of its real causes and issues, a consistent regard for British principles, and a spirit of honourable patience under severe trials, which ought to shame most of its hereditary and elected rulers.

The two great arguments used in England in favour of Southern independence are, that thereby the power of the United States will be divided—one of the fragments, the Southern Confederacy, becoming the friend and ally of England; and that a direct free-trade with the South will be established. Let us look a moment at the merits of these considerations.

In the debate in the House of Lords, March 23, 1863, the mover,

[1] Speech of Earl Russell in the House of Lords, March 23d, 1863.

in favour of recognising the South urged that, "Great Britain requires an ally on the other side of the Atlantic, and that ally the North could not furnish, not from any difference of interest or feelings of antipathy as regards England," but *because* the United States is the offspring of a successful revolt against England. Now, we venture to say that a shallower reason for so important a policy, as the one proposed, was never given; and, moreover, it assumes that the Southern colonies did not revolt against British supremacy, as well as the Northern.

Every one who knows anything of the state of public sentiment in the United States knows that, ever since the British Emancipation Act, and the declarations of the British Government and people against slavery in general, as indicative of a settled policy, England has had no friend in the Slave States. Every well-informed man knows that all the diplomatic or other manifestations of hostility on the part of the United States Government have been the expressions of this Southern anti-English feeling, easily assuming the form of a national exhibition because the South has been supreme in the national administration. Every one knows that, throughout the Free States—excepting amongst the Irish settlers and, perhaps, the ultra-democratic German immigrants—a feeling far different from hostility to England pervades the people. The common origin, the community of laws, literature, and religion, the constant and increasing interchange of ideas and products between the two nations are appreciated by the people of the North, and had obliterated all those unfriendly feelings which the early international wars had engendered, and had substituted for them a feeling of amity and kinship for the English people.[1] No better or more conclusive evidence of this can be needed than the reception everywhere given, in the Free States, to the Prince of Wales. He was there treated more like a sovereign on a royal progress through his own dominions and

[1] We venture to say that all observing English travellers in the Free States will confirm this statement. Mr. Stirling, writing in 1856, says, "I was astonished to find so little hostility to England, even among the lower order of Americans; excepting in the diatribes of some obscure Democratic paper, or the spouting of some ex-rebel, or ex-revolutionist, I scarcely saw a trace of it," p. 356. And as regards the public feeling of hostility to England during the Crimean War, which some English journals have made so much of, Mr. Stirling says that a friend of his, who happened to be in a theatre in Boston when the manager came upon the stage and announced the fall of Sebastopol, assured him that the whole audience arose and cheered, and demanded "God Save the Queen," p. 210.

amongst his own loyal subjects, than as a stranger prince amidst a people over whom his fathers had once ruled. But, in the first place he visited in the Slave States he was publicly insulted. Even the mover of the resolution to recognise the Southern confederacy, was compelled to acknowledge that the Northern States had "no difference of interests or feelings of antipathy as regards England." He well knew that the States of the Confederacy, or their people, had both; and that the contrary professions which they have made since their rebellion are assumed simply to gain English assistance, and will be dropped so soon as they fail of their object, or shall be no longer necessary. No sensible Englishman, who knows anything of the real sentiments of the Southern people towards England, can imagine that there can be any lasting or beneficial alliance between the two, unless the former be assisted to foster and extend their slavery interests. But who can pretend that an alliance, even if it do not involve this concession on the part of England, with a mere fragment of the former Union—and this, as we have shown, the poorest and the least progressive of the two sections—can compare in its substantial and ever-increasing benefits with that which has subsisted with the entire nation? Has not England directly and immensely benefited hitherto by every event which has increased the prosperity of the United States? Is it not certain that any check to that prosperity must re-act unfavourably upon Great Britain? An alliance between these is not an alliance between the two Governments merely, but between the two peoples of a common origin and of kindred interests. Or, if a choice must be made between the North and the South, it requires no prophet to foretel that an alliance with the former will be infinitely more beneficial to England than with the latter. What permanent profit, what lasting friendship, can be hoped for between a people which has so long and so loudly proclaimed its hostility to slavery, and this new association of States which have—without just cause of offence, and for the sole perpetuation of negro slavery—wilfully broken through all their constitutional obligations and all the ties of a common nationality? By what new obligations, by what ties of interest stronger than these—unless by the furtherance of slavery—can England hope to bind the "Slave Republic"?

Moreover, it is the Northern section which has the power—

or, at least, the facilities, if it had the disposition and the desire—to disturb the peace of Great Britain, through her North American possessions. Thus, an alliance with the Free States, which is of direct and immediate importance to England and her colonies in America, between which and them a constant intercourse and commerce is carried on, and which was already established on a sure foundation of respect and good feeling on the part of the Northern American people, and on the immense and increasing commercial and personal relations between the two nations—this certain alliance is endangered and well-nigh sacrificed for a mere possible contingency imagined and advocated by political schemers and commercial speculators.

In the second place, can the Southern Confederacy, in the event of the independence of a few of its original States, aid in the realization of the free-trade dream of British merchants and manufacturers?

We have seen that a tariff "for the support of Government, for the discharge of the public debt, and for the encouragement and protection of manufactures," was originally imposed upon the United States under the lead of the South; and that a tariff for the creation of a revenue has always been a favourite measure with the Slave States, and for the reasons which we have explained. Will the Southern Confederacy be likely to adopt a different policy now, when a public debt, far greater than ever before pressed upon the whole Union, will tax the utmost resources of the poorest and least progressive fragment of it? We have seen that the South refused to submit to direct taxation, under the Union, on account of its oppressiveness, as compared with the means of the Southern people. Will it be more likely to submit thereto now that a prolonged war has shattered its whole industrial system, and limited its territory to the oldest and most worn-out of the Slave States?

Moreover, Southern legislation is in the hands of the planters. Is it not self-evident that these will endeavour to develope the natural resources of their country, by favouring the establishment of manufacturing and mining interests and industries (the need of which the war has abundantly taught), in order that their own class shall not alone be compelled to support the State? And to accomplish this, will not a high-tariff system be absolutely necessary?

Again, the Confederacy will require a navy; and how can a

navy be maintained without a commercial marine? Hence a necessity will arise for the fostering of a Southern shipping interest.

Thus, from every consideration, the Confederacy will be compelled, in self-defence, to resort to the same means of building up its own resources of all kinds which England and every other nation have employed, in their infancy, and under whose protecting care the resources of Great Britain have become among the wonders of the world. And this system of protection will be especially necessary to the South, because its population is more deficient in all those requisites for self-sustentation and progress than any other modern civilized people, under its present slavery *régime.* It will begin its national career under the burthen of a debt of fabulous proportions, compared with its resources. It must incur immense annual expenses to maintain all the varied machinery of an independent government—its civil list, its military and naval power, its customs and post-office departments, the lighting of its coasts, the maintenance of its harbours, &c. &c. Of all these incumbrances, the Slave States, as we have seen, bore less than one-fourth of the weight, under the Union, and were, even then, comparatively retrograding and absolutely impoverished. So far, then, from being able to sacrifice its own interests to the advantage of British manufacturers and shippers, the Confederacy must subject these to stringent customs' regulations; and, in addition, it must levy a tax upon all its exports of cotton and tobacco.

But, even supposing free-trade to be established, of what great advantage will it be to Great Britain, to compensate for all the probable losses to which British trade will be subjected, in consequence of the ill-feeling or animosity engendered at the North by Southern independence, gained through English connivance and aid? We have seen the wretched condition of the mass of the Southern population. We have shown that slavery, while it has enriched a few thousand planters and their agents and brokers, has reduced the millions to "hopeless ignorance and poverty." Can we hope for improvement, when the Confederacy shall have become independent upon the exclusive basis of slavery, and when all the expenses of a separate government shall come to be borne by a reduced population, daily becoming more impoverished? All the ordinary articles of manufacture needed by the mass of the Southern population have hitherto been furnished from the North, and must continue to be sought thence, as from the nearest and cheapest market. Will the small residue left to be supplied from England and all Europe compensate the former for all the disadvantages of its new alliance, and for the loss, or the diminished value, of its hitherto best customer?

We say nothing about the *morality* of the new alliance. We have discussed its value upon the pound, shilling, and pence standard of its British advocates. And we believe that, even upon this basis, England has been made to commit a gross blunder by those who have been allowed to shape its policy towards the United States.

The idea is diligently disseminated that slavery is already destroyed, and that if the Confederacy should become independent it will be as a free republic. Let not the anti-slavery men of Great Britain allow themselves to be deceived by this artful assurance of the Southern advocates. If only those States of the Confederacy lying east of the Mississippi should become independent, comprising only the eastern part of Virginia, the Carolinas, Georgia, Alabama, Florida, and Mississippi, they will embrace territory and population enough for a considerable State. It must be borne in mind that, during the war, thousands of slaves have been removed from the Border States to the cotton-growing States for safety from Federal troops; so that the slave-population of the States we have named is greater now than before the war, and vastly more numerous as compared with the whites, whom the war has decimated. And of the 331,711 square miles, or 212,295,040 acres, of territory embraced within those States, only some 36,000,000 acres were under cultivation in 1860, leaving still untouched 176,295,000 acres—*an area larger than that of France, England, and Wales combined.* It is idle, therefore, to suppose that a country so extensive as this, possessing natural resources so great, capable of producing a crop of cotton sufficient to keep in operation all the cotton mills of the world, with a slave force larger than it ever owned before, and ruled by men whose ability and energy, and whose determination to uphold slavery, will have carried the Confederacy triumphantly through the war—we say it is idle to suppose that such a State, if it become independent, will not live out its national life as a "slave republic." Who shall say, too, that the new power may not possess itself of Cuba, and thus add to its resources and its territory? The leading men of the Confederacy have, as we know, long coveted, and frequently attempted to possess themselves of, this island; with a large military force at their own command, and possessed of a navy created in British ports—aided, too, by disaffected planters in Cuba—the possibility of conquering the island would be sufficiently encouraging to induce the attempt.

We say, therefore, that if the Confederate States do become independent, they will constitute a "slave republic," or a slave power under some other name. Any aid or encouragement from England, or from Englishmen, will only contribute to the accomplishment of this end, which the Southern leaders proclaimed from the first to be their great object, and which they have never ceased to keep in view.

It is really curious to examine some of the many charges which have been brought against the United States Government and the people of the Free States, in order to create an odium against them in England, under cover of which the true policy, which both principle and interest should have dictated to Great Britain towards them, might be ignored or unheeded.

We pass over the stale slanders so often uttered against us of *barbarism*, *cruelty*, and the like. Those who believe these fictions, and who wish to find a refutation of the same, will find them abundantly answered in the able speech of Senator Sumner on Our Foreign Relations, delivered in New York, in September, 1863. We would also refer honest inquirers to the reports and records of the United States Sanitary Commission—an association which had, up to the close of 1863, expended more than a million of dollars, and seven millions' worth of supplies of various sorts, all voluntary contributions, in the relief of the sick, the wounded, and the suffering, not only of the United States military forces, but also of those of the Confederate Government, without distinction, as well as all the needy inhabitants of the South who have come within the sphere of its action.

We pass over likewise the plea that England's favour is shown to the "Slave Republic" because this is the weaker party in the contest, and Englishmen always side with the feeble. *Credat Judæus.* England has been fighting, in some quarter or other of the globe, for a century, with some poor but brave tribe which, *pro aris et focis,* has contended against her armies as courageously as the Southerners now fight in behalf of slavery. At this moment, British troops are combating with varying success against some wretched tribes in New Zealand.

An assertion which British orators in and out of Parliament seem to be still fond of repeating is, that the seizure of the *Trent*, and the removal from it of the Southern Commissioners, was a wanton and predetermined act of the Government of the United States, and that the latter only made reparation for the act upon the threats of the British Government. Now, it is well known that Mr. Seward's despatch to Mr. Adams, which declared that the American Government had not authorized that seizure, regretted it, and was willing to make any suitable reparation for it, was dated on the same day as the British demand for restitution and satisfaction. But one of the prominent London journals, which has the reputation of being a semi-official organ of the Premier, did not hesitate at the time to invent two deliberate falsehoods—first, denying that the American minister had received any such despatch, and, secondly, asserting that he had not communicated it to the British Government. Meanwhile, the howl for war was encouraged, and re-echoed, according to the journals of the time, from the pulpit of at least one of the fashionable London churches.

That seizure was entirely contrary to the doctrine of the United States from its origin as a nation. And the reason why the Commissioners taken from the *Trent* were not released without waiting for the British demand for restoration was simply in order that Great Britain—which as a belligerent had always treated neutrals ruthlessly, from seizing a whole fleet at Copenhagen, to impressing seamen by hundreds from American ships—should, as a neutral, place on record in the archives at Washington a full, formal, and official recognition of the rights of neutrals.

Another gross violation of historical truth, and of the truths of English history as well, is in the attempt to fasten upon *Republican Institutions* the especial odium of this war, and of the many evils which have accompanied it. How can any thoughtful and intelligent Englishman imagine that he has found in English history any warrant for the assertion that Monarchism, constitutional or otherwise, has been more incompatible with, or less promotive of, war and lavish expenditure, of political immorality and corruption, of judicial venality, of utter worthlessness and incapacity, from the highest to the lowest personages, than democratic republicanism?

And here we insist that it is eminently unjust to hold "the American system of politics" responsible either for this war, or for the train of evils which have attended it. For we have had implanted and growing up in our midst, a system which is diametrically opposite to ours—the aristocratic, oligarchic system of the Slave States—which has completely ruled its own section of the country, and swayed the policy of the whole nation. Like an immense and baneful planet which deviates the majestic march of the earth itself, this disturbing element has drawn the American Constitution astray from its normal and intended orbit.

This charge against American institutions was made, in a particularly marked and offensive way, by no less a personage than the British Premier. In his speech soliciting from the House of Commons a suitable appanage for the Prince and Princess of Wales, he thought it necessary, it would seem, to stimulate their loyalty and liberality by making an otherwise most uncalled-for and indecorous attack upon America. He told his audience of "the wide-spread misery and desolation *created* in the West by democratic and republican institutions. Our institutions," he continued, "our institutions[1] not only

[1] Far be it from us to detract from the merits of British institutions. We love England, as the land of great deeds done, and of wise lessons taught, in behalf of human progress; as the cradle of our own nation, the *fons et origo* of our own literature, laws, liberties, and religion. We well remember the feeling of almost reverence which impelled us, on first setting foot upon her soil, to raise our hat in salutation. We regret that Englishmen, in expressing their satisfaction with their own institutions, should so generally decry those of other lands. It is in no spirit of fault-finding or of controversy, but in defence of our own chosen systems of politics and government, that we submit the following comparative statements, from authorities which Englishmen cannot accuse of *Anglophobia.* The first is from an interesting work on "The Social Condition and Education of the People in England and Europe," by Joseph Kay, Esq. M.A. Trinity Coll. Cambridge, who was appointed by the University to examine the above subject. His book is made up from official statistics and reports, and from personal investigation. At the commencement of the first volume, Mr. Kay says: "If the object of Government be to create an enormously wealthy class, and to raise to the highest pitch the civilization of about one-fifth of the nation, while it leaves nearly three-fifths sunk in the lowest depths of ignorance, hopelessness, and degradation, then the system hitherto pursued in Great Britain is perfect; for the classes of our aristocracy, our landed gentry, our merchants, manufacturers, and richer tradespeople, are wealthier, more refined in their tastes, more active and enterprising, more intelligent, and consequently more prosperous, than the corresponding classes of any other country in the world."—Vol. i. p. 6.

Mr. Kay sums up the result of his studies in the following words:—"Here, where the poor have no stake whatever in the country; where there are no small properties; where the most frightful discrepancy exists between the richer and poorer classes; where the poor fancy they have nothing to lose and everything to

confer happiness and tranquillity upon the people of these realms, but enable them to enjoy the most perfect freedom of thought, of speech, of writing, and action, and all undeterred by the edicts of despotic authority, or the Lynch-law of an ungovernable mob." Is not every candid person reminded by this effusion of the Pharisee in the Temple thanking God that he is not as other men, or even as these republicans? Every Englishman must know that no political institutions have passed through so many revolutions as his own; that no land, excepting France in her great Revolution, has been the theatre of such terrible mobs as England; that no English Government ever has ever hesitated, or ever will hesitate, to suspend the Habeas Corpus Act, the right to freedom of writing, of speech, and of action, or any other right, whenever, in its judgment, the state of the country, or any particular part of it, has required, or shall hereafter require, such suspension. This was done in the last small rebellion in Ireland, as the Foreign Secretary admitted; and how thoroughly and generally it was done during the English war with France, Lord Macaulay has shown in his account of Mr. Pitt's administration.

Lynch-law is almost one of the "peculiar institutions" of the Slave States, where an Abolitionist, or a suspected Abolitionist, or a negro who has, in self-defence or otherwise, committed some desperate act, is hung, or burned, or whipped to death.

gain from a revolution; here, where we are stimulating the rapid increase of our population by extending and steadying the base of our commercial greatness; where the majority of the operatives have no religion; where the national religion is one utterly unfitted to attract an uneducated people; where our very freedom is a danger, unless the people are taught to use and not to abuse it; and here, too, where the aristocracy is richer and more powerful than that of any other country in the world;—*the poor are more depressed, more pauperised, more numerous in comparison with the other classes, more irreligious, and very much worse educated, than the poor of any other European nation, solely excepting Russia, Turkey, South Italy, Portugal, and Spain.*"—Vol. ii. last page. The italics are of Mr. Kay's own making. This is an Englishman's picture of the results of British institutions, which Lord Palmerston praises in opposition to the democratic republican institutions of the United States.

The other authority which we shall cite is the London *Times*, 1859, which thus speaks of that portion of the United States which furnishes the best example of the workings of democratic and republican institutions, because these have been less affected there by the influence of Southern slavery and of foreign immigration. The *Times* says:—"No community of which we have any knowledge approaches, in enlightenment and morality, to the New England States; where, though wealth is not piled up in masses, as in New York, yet poverty hardly exists, education is universal, and the tone of society is singularly high-minded and liberal."

We desire no better refutation of the calumny of Lord Palmerston than is afforded by the comparison of these two statements.

Mobs, concerning which we have been favoured with so many extraordinary assertions and predictions by English journalists, are almost unknown to us, excepting amongst the foreign population of some of our largest cities. Considering that we have had no standing military force, and scarce any *police*, as Europeans understand the expression, the almost uniform absence of lawless violence, even amongst our foreign population, is wonderfully suggestive of the humanising and improving effects of our institutions upon them.[1] In their own land, most of these constituted what Mr. Roebuck would call *the scum, the mob;* they come to the United States, and they quickly lose their lawless propensities. Why? Because we treat them as rational and intelligent beings, we acknowledge their natural rights, we give them privileges, we hold out to them the sure prospect of improvement and advancement, we insure freely to their children and themselves the means of instruction, and they become useful and prosperous members of the community.

Again, the management of our military affairs has called forth a good deal of derision amongst Englishmen. But England should be the last country in the world to make merry over the alleged incompetency of United States officials in the conduct of a great war. Her own annals are filled with what, under the comparative circumstances of the two nations, are much more glaring examples of real incapacity. We need only refer to English accounts of the Crimean war, as the latest instance, for our proofs. The vast extent of territory over which our war is spread; the immense proportions of the war; the wildness of the country, the utter absence of good roads, its capabilities of defence; the want of military experience, the size of the armies to be raised and equipped, with scarce a nucleus for such forces when the war began; the character of our enemies—brave, determined, fighting on the defensive on ground with which they were thoroughly acquainted, possessing a body of slaves to perform all the necessary work at home, while the entire white

[1] There was one common trait in the natural history of the only three *mobs*, which, so far as we remember, have made any mark upon the page of the last three years; and this common feature is not a little curious in this connexion. The first, made up of Britons, occurred at Staleybridge, in England, in 1862; the second, composed of British subjects recently landed at New York, occurred in that city, in July, 1863; and the third, likewise made up of British subjects, signalized itself at Halifax, on British ground, by rescuing from the hands of the police the pirates of the Chesapeake, which they had captured during the present year.

population has been forced to fight; every officer from almost the lowest to the highest rank, not only in the army, but in the civil administration, being a slave-holder, and, consequently, personally interested in the success of the rebellion, and accustomed almost from his infancy to the blind respect and obedience of all of inferior social rank;—all these considerations have been overlooked by our English critics.

We are told that our armies are made up chiefly of foreigners. There are, indeed, many soldiers and officers of foreign birth in our armies. And why not? They are citizens of the Republic, as well as the natives of the land.[1] But there is scarcely a family of position, education, and wealth, from Maine to Maryland, from Delaware to California (besides the thousands of industrious, respectable, and prosperous working men), which has not sent its representatives to the field of battle. They are all animated by a sincere love for their country, its constitution and its union; that same love of country, under the full influence of which the dying Spartan boy was borne proudly homeward on his bloody shield, and laid with a song of triumph on the threshold of his mother's cottage; that noble love of country which prompted the stern epitaph of the gallant Brasidas: "Sparta hath many a worthier son than he;" they are our *Curtii,* who plunge into the yawning gulf of rebellion to save their fatherland. God bless them!

We shall notice only one more charge made against us; but this is a very important one. It is said that, at the beginning of the war, slavery was not at all involved as a cause or an issue. The English Foreign Secretary, whose liberality we honour, declared, in words which have become famous, "The North is fighting for supremacy, and the South for independence." And so it is, or, rather, so it was: the North was fighting for supremacy, and in that supremacy of the Union the South clearly saw the gradual but sure overthrow of slavery, and, therefore, seceded. The South is fighting for independence, but it is for independence of all restraint upon the permanence and extension of slavery—it is for freedom to enslave.

One of the peculiarities of the United States Constitution has been, very naturally, unknown or overlooked in England.

[1] We have not the proportions of natives and foreigners in our armies. But Mr. Caird lately stated in the House of Commons that, being recently in Illinois, he found that, in the regiments enlisted in that State (in which the foreign population is very large), 60 per cent. were Americans. (*Daily News,* March 15th.)

Englishmen reason, because the British Parliament abolished slavery in the West India Islands, the American Congress can, if it see fit, abolish slavery in the Southern States. But the functions and powers of the two Parliaments are unequal. The British Parliament is *supreme* over all the realm; the jurisdiction of the United States Congress is *limited* by the Constitution to matters which concern the general interests of the whole country. Slavery is an institution local to each State, and is subject only to State legislation; only in the territories and in the district of Columbia had the Congress any right to meddle with it.

The history of the United States, particularly during the last seven or eight years, shows conclusively that the North has been opposed to slavery, has been desirous, in every lawful way, to prevent its extension, and thus gradually to overthrow it. Mr. Fremont was voted for in 1856, and almost elected President, simply because he and the party which supported him were determined to limit slavery. Mr. Lincoln was elected upon the same ground. The mere fact of his election was evidence of itself that the North had determined to limit slavery under the Union; the South understood the meaning of that election, and left the Union to found a new government, under which slavery should be perpetual. The real meaning of Mr. Lincoln's election was as well understood by intelligent men and leading journalists in England, as it was either in the Northern or Southern States of the Union. This is evident, as we have already remarked, from the extracts we have before given from the *Times*.

There is one declaration of the President which has been strangely misinterpreted in England, viz. that it was his duty to maintain the Constitution with slavery, if this should be possible, without it, if its destruction should become necessary. And clearly this was his duty. He was bound by his inaugural oath to uphold the Constitution as the supreme law of the land; that Constitution allowed of the existence of slavery in the States, under State laws; it was only when that institution and those laws came into conflict with the supreme law which the President was bound to uphold and enforce, and only to the degree of that conflict, that he could be at all warranted in interfering with the institution. And so he has honestly endeavoured to fulfil his duty. The more one considers the difficulties which the President has had to encounter from enemies without, and lukewarm friends and traitors within; viewing the delicacy of his position between the loyal slave-holding States and the Slave States in rebellion—between the necessity of conciliating the constitutional rights of the former with the stern demands made upon him by the military power of the latter—we say, in view of these and other similar considerations, Mr. Lincoln and his government deserve immense praise for what they have thus far accomplished, and for the wise and prudent and liberal measures which they have adopted.

It may suit the narrow minds and the illiberal policy of certain men and certain classes or parties in England and elsewhere, to sneer at Mr. Lincoln for his humble origin, and for his want of what is ordinarily called a liberal education; and to speak contemptuously of the institutions of a country which has placed such a man in its chief magistracy. Mr. Lincoln is a man of sound sense; of unexceptionable morality; of undenied honesty and integrity of character and purpose; of remarkable practical tact in discerning "the signs of the times;" of clear perceptions as to the extent and limits of his official powers, which he honestly wishes neither to exceed nor to come short of; and if there be any selfishness in his ambition it is only that of desiring to carry out to its legitimate end the policy which he has aided to inaugurate, and which, he believes, is most likely to secure the permanent welfare of his country. There is no European nation, however long its line of kings or kaisers, which can show many of them who have possessed this combination of desiderata in a ruler. Mr. Lincoln's education he has acquired amidst such difficulties as none but a man of original capability and strong will, accompanied by an earnest desire to learn, would have surmounted; the education thus gained has been gradually developed in a practical school of constant expansion and promotion. And we venture to predict that his name and titles, "Rail-splitter," "Bargee," Country Attorney, Congressman, President of the United States, Emancipator of four millions of slaves, will be honoured in history, when his detractors—polished *gentlemen*, crafty politicians—will be forgotten, or remembered only to be damned.

Since the war began, and step by step with its progress, the anti-slavery sentiment of the Free States has declared and manifested itself more decidedly and more actively. At first, it only demanded the non-extension of slavery; the Constitution would not sanction anything more. But the armed rebellion of the South cut the constitutional knot which philanthropists have been unable to untie, and which politicians had only drawn tighter. War exacted as a necessity what the Constitution could not authorize as a right, and the President's proclamation abolished slavery, technically, in the revolted States, leaving the institution to the operation of natural and inevitable causes of decay in the loyal Slave States.

And now let us enumerate the great facts by which the Free States and the United States Government have exhibited their anti-slavery principles:—

1. The election of a President pledged to the non-extension of slavery, 1860.

2. Congress abolished slavery in the district of Columbia (compensating loyal owners); provided for the education of coloured children within the district, and established within it the equality of all persons before the criminal law, 1862.

3. Congress abolished slavery in all the territories of the United States, " in order that freedom shall be the natural inheritance of the inhabitants thereof for ever."

4. The assistance of the national treasury has been promised to any State which shall ask it, after having enacted emancipation laws to take effect within a certain time.

5. Great Britain has been empowered to search all vessels bearing the United States flag, suspected of being engaged in the slave-trade.

6. The Republics of Hayti and Liberia have been acknowledged, and their ambassadors have been received at Washington.

7. A new sanction has been given to the law against the slave-trade by the execution of a convicted slave-trader.

8. The President's proclamation announcing freedom to all the slaves in States in revolt, 1863.

9. The enrolment into the civil and military service of free negroes and freed slaves.

Surely, never since God led the children of Israel out of Egypt, has the march of a people from slavery to freedom been so rapid and so certain.

It has been objected to the President's proclamation of enfranchisement that it was insincere, because it limited its operation to those slaves who were still in the power of their masters, in States as yet unoccupied by Federal troops, while those who might at any time be freed by the Union forces were left in bondage. Again, it was stigmatised as a barbarous attempt to instigate a servile insurrection. This last assertion was sufficiently refuted by the very circumstances of the case; for where there were no United States troops to prevent any attempt at insurrection, there were Southern soldiers. But the event has thus far proved that no such result has followed the proclamation.

The objection as to the insincerity of the proclamation has been sufficiently answered by our reference to the Constitution. And, moreover, the enfranchisement of the slaves in the loyal States had been provided for by the offer of compensation already stated. The rapidity with which emancipation has progressed and is progressing in these States is not the least noteworthy event in this great struggle. The larger part of Virginia, Missouri, and Louisiana have already adopted emancipation measures; Maryland, and Tennessee, and Delaware, and Arkansas have taken preliminary steps towards the same great object; Kentucky must follow rapidly. In short, in all but the remote cotton-growing States, the fate of slavery is already decided.

Thus we see that, long before the war, the North had begun in earnest to restore to the Constitution the image of liberty which its founders had impressed upon it, but which had become effaced or defaced by "the greed" of Southern slave-holders, and Northern sycophants and place-hunters.

The results already accomplished, and others similar, which these foreshadow, could, unhappily, have been accomplished, humanly speaking, only by the war. And when the work shall have been completed, who shall say—as so many persist in proclaiming now—that the war has been useless and in vain? We read the future very differently. We see the South immeasurably enriched by the loss of what she has hitherto considered her peculiar blessing, her richest jewel. We see, as the darkness of slavery vanishes before the dawn of a brighter day (and we believe that those who have read our statements of the comparative results of freedom and slavery, as exhibited at the North and South respectively, will not deem the vision false or supernatural)—we see her population increased by the advent of industrious, skilful, and hopeful labourers. We see a thriving and intelligent middle-class growing up. We see the fertile soil increased in value, and yielding more abounding and more varied harvests. We see her cities enlarging and multiplying, and becoming the marts of commerce and the centres of manufacturing industry. We see her mines yielding up their treasures. We see churches and school-houses multiplying, and diffusing through every home of rich and poor the advantages, the comforts, the treasures, the glorious hopes which education and religion alone can impart. And we see the blight and bane which Southerners themselves admit had settled down upon their land, expiated and removed.

As to the North, the enormous material sacrifices which the war has occasioned will be amply compensated by an increased and a more healthful prosperity. The blood of her children slain in this most righteous cause will be recompensed in blessings. The reapers will return from these fields of slaughter, bearing with them, to their peaceful homes, sheaves of glory purer and more enduring than that of ordinary conquerors: the curse which had been concealed amidst all her material riches will have been withdrawn, and her sons, chastened by sufferings, will become wiser and better citizens of a more glorious republic.

And what will become of the freed slaves? They will remain where "the ignoble love of gold" of their former masters had placed them. But they will remain to reap a fair reward for their labour; and, by their more cheerful and more productive industry, they will aid in bringing prosperity upon the land which hitherto, by a just retribution, they had cursed.

The assertion of Southerners, that the whites and the freed slaves will not be able to inhabit the same country, will, by the very necessities of the case, be disproved. For by whom is the land to be cultivated? The poor non-slaveholding whites, accustomed to regard field-labour as degrading, will not speedily acquire more just views and more industrious habits. Hence the freed slaves will be—at least for some years to come—the only available labourers, and they will be by far the most docile and respectful whom the planters can employ. Moreover, the experience of other countries in which slavery has been abolished, and of our own Free States, shows that the above objection, always put forward in similar cases, has no real weight or foundation in experience.[1]

[1] It is important to notice here, that the most dense negro population in the country is in Maryland, and that the most dense free negro population in that State is in Frederick County, which is its most populous and prosperous

The pretence that the freed slave will not work is contrary not only to experience, but to nature and to common sense. The common instincts of humanity are, at least, as strong in the black as in the white man. Necessity will beget industry and prudence, and these will create comfort and improvement. The labourer, finding himself necessary to his employer, will gradually learn that the latter must acknowledge and respect his *rights;* and, in turn, the planter will perceive that his own interests are bound up with the welfare and the happiness of the negro. Thus a sentiment of mutual dependence will spring up between the two, to the advantage of both.

These are not mere speculations. It has long been known that the negroes, while slaves, have worked better and more profitably to the master when the prospect of reward has been held before them. The slaves of a well-known planter in Louisiana not only accomplished all their allotted task, but purchased their own freedom as the reward of extra work. Since the war began, the freed slaves have everywhere worked as hired labourers far better than they ever did as slaves.[1]

county. There is no complaint made by the farmers there of bad conduct on the part of those negroes; on the contrary, they are indispensable to the farmers. There is double the number of free negroes to the square mile in Maryland and Delaware than there is of slaves, on the average, in the whole cotton region of the South; and they are vastly more industrious and more profitable members of the community, than the mass of the non-slaveholding whites of the Slave States. ("Boston Trade Report," pp. 111, 112.)

[1] We quote the following conclusive evidence on this point from the "Report on the Condition and Management of the Emancipated Negroes in the United States," *Daily News*, Sept. 25th, 1863: "Mr. Frederick A. Eustis, son of General Eustis, who owned the plantation on Ladies' Island, South Carolina, and who has returned to cultivate that plantation by hired labour, while expressing the opinion, that the new system of labour in Carolina is too lenient, gave the following testimony as to the people now working on his own plantation: 'I never knew, during forty years of plantation life, so little sickness. Formerly, every man had a fever of some kind, and now the veriest old cripple, who did nothing before, will row a boat three nights in succession to Edisto, or will pick up the corn about the corn-house. There are twenty people whom I know were considered worn-out and too old to work under the slave system, who are now working cotton, as well as their own two acres of provisions; and their crops look very well. I have an old woman who has taken six tasks (that is, an acre and a half) of cotton, and last year she would do nothing.'" In short, the universal testimony corresponds with the above. Captain Hooper, the acting superintendent of the post at Hilton Head, having charge of some 17,000 freed slaves, testified that he "never knew a case in which a coloured man had reasonable security for getting wages—even moderate wages—that he did not work." "In the city of Washington, which contains 16,000 free negroes, these support their own poor without almshouse aid, and there is scarcely a beggar amongst them."

The evidence given to the United States Commissioners, appointed to examine into and report upon the condition and necessities of the slaves whom the war had freed, shows that the latter are more willing to help themselves than are the poor whites of the South. In November, 1862, General Butler was giving rations to 32,000 whites, 17,000 of whom were born in Great Britain, while only 10,000 negroes presented themselves for similar aid; and most of the latter were women and children, the able-bodied men being usually employed on abandoned plantations.

The vices most common amongst the negroes are such as were naturally and necessarily developed by slavery; and there is abundant evidence to show that these same vices are equally prevalent amongst the poor whites of the South, whom the same system has degraded and debased.

The Commissioners were struck with "the high value which the freedmen in general place both on education for their children and religious instruction for themselves. In Alexandria, and in various other places, one of the first acts of the negroes, when they found themselves free, was to establish schools at their own expense; and in every instance where schools and churches have been provided for them they have shown lively gratitude and the greatest eagerness to avail themselves of such opportunities of improvement."

The general conclusion of the Commissioners is as follows: "The observations of the Commission in the sections of country visited by them, together with the evidence obtained from those having most experience of freedmen, justify the conclusion that the African race, as found among us, lacks no essential aptitude for civilization. In general, the negro yields willingly to its restraints, and enters upon its duties, not only with alacrity, but with evident pride and increase of self-respect. His personal rights as a freedman once recognised in law and assured in practice, there is little reason to doubt that he will become a useful member of the great industrial family of nations." Meantime the Government is making every exertion to fulfil its share of duty in carrying out the great experiment now begun; and it is aided by the benevolent and religious societies, as well as by individuals, in the Free States, to secure not only the material prosperity of the freedmen, but their intellectual and moral training.

Those who oppose the abolition of slavery point triumphantly to what they call *the failure* of the English emancipation policy in the West Indies. We, on the contrary, appeal to that with great confidence as an unanswerable argument in favour of the substitution there made of free for slave labour. The chief reason why the British experiment did not succeed as completely as it might have succeeded, was that the short-sighted, selfish policy of the planters themselves prevented complete success. But, even estimated in rum and sugar—the standard by which that great national Act of Emancipation has always been weighed by its high-minded decriers,—the experiment has succeeded.

In four of the five principal British West India colonies—Guiana, Trinidad, Barbados, and Antigua,—the total average annual export of sugar during the four years preceding emancipation was 187,300,000lbs.; the average annual export from 1856 to 1860, was 265,000,000lbs. This gives an excess of export, under free labour, of 77,700,000lbs. of sugar alone. The total annual average of imports to these islands, from 1820 to 1834, was of the value of $8,840,000, against a total value of $14,600,000 in 1859. If all the other articles of export were included besides sugar, it is estimated that the average annual balance in favour of freedom, since emancipation, would be at least $15,000,000.

And it must be remembered that this increased production of sugar in those four islands is due to the labour of about half the number of labourers, as compared with the days of slavery; showing an improved system of agriculture, or a greater amount of individual work, or both. One of the most natural and legitimate results of emancipation was that every man consulted his own choice or opportunities as to the employment of his labour. In all the islands, but especially in Jamaica, where land was abundant and cheap, very many of the freed slaves betook themselves, as soon as possible, to small holdings, which they purchased and cultivated for themselves—thus diminishing to a very considerable extent the labour devoted to sugar-culture, and diffusing it in the cultivation of numerous products of comparatively small value for each, but swelling the aggregate production greatly, and securing to each small proprietor independence, comfort, happiness, and a degree of self-respect which he had never possessed before.

In Barbados, where labour is very abundant, the population being in the ratio of one and a half inhabitant to each acre of land, and where the price of land is $500 per acre, one would suppose that there could be but little chance of a freed slave becoming a landed proprietor. And yet, even in Barbados, where the field-labourer gets but about twenty-four cents per day, the number of proprietors holding less than five acres has, within the last fifteen years, increased from 1,100 to 3,537. Most of these were formerly slaves, then paid labourers, and finally landholders.

In St. Vincent, in 1857, no less than 8,209 freedmen were living in their own houses, built by themselves since emancipation. And during the last twelve years from ten to twelve thousand acres of land, in holdings of from one to five acres, have been brought under cultivation by these small proprietors, who produce arrow-root, vegetables, &c. for export. There are no paupers on the island. In the one article of arrow-root alone there were exported, in 1857, 1,352,250lbs. valued at $750,000, against an average yearly export of 60,000lbs. before emancipation.

In Granada, the small proprietors, of whom there were none before emancipation, now number over 2,000, and are greatly increasing; nearly 7,000 persons are living in villages built since emancipation; and there are 4,573 of these freedmen who pay direct taxes.

In Trinidad, of the 11,000 negroes set free, about 4,000 remained on the estates, working at low wages. Of the remainder, about five-sixths have become proprietors of from one to ten acres of land each, upon which, with the aid of occasional labour on estates, they make an independent support for themselves and their families.

In morality there is said to be a marked improvement amongst the negroes since emancipation, although the means of religious and intellectual training afforded them have been disgracefully small.

The cost of free-labour as compared with slave-labour is found to be less than one half, estimating the expenses of sugar-production under each system.[1]

The condition of Jamaica since emancipation is the *cheval de bataille* of the anti-abolitionists, who say that the sugar-interest

[1] Sewell, "The Ordeal of Free Labour in the British West Indies," London, 1862, *passim.*

and, consequently, the prosperity of the island (the culture of the sugar-cane being then its only interest), were ruined by emancipation. It would be nearer the truth to say that this interest was almost ruined before emancipation; that this catastrophe was completed by the removal of the almost prohibitive duties on slave-grown sugars imported into England; and that the prosperity of the island, under the new and much more economical labour system introduced by emancipation, might have been revived and secured, had not the opportunity been abused and disdainfully ~~ejected~~ by the planters.

It is well known that, long before the abolition of slavery was dreamed of in England, the sugar estates of Jamaica had begun to decline, owing to heavy incumbrances, want of capital, mismanagement, extravagance, absenteeism on the part of the proprietors, who committed everything to agents at a large discount of profits, &c. In 1792, the Jamaica Assembly reported that within twenty years 177 estates had been sold for debt; in 1807, the same body declared that, in the five years preceding the abolition of the slave-trade, 65 estates had been abandoned. In 1831, a convention of delegates from all the islands met in Barbados to impress upon Parliament "the very urgent necessity which exists for immediate and substantial relief to save them from impending ruin." The relief which they sought was *the re-opening of the slave-trade,* without which, they said, they could not compete in the sugar culture with the Spanish islands, which continued to enjoy that blessing. During the seven years preceding the abolition of the slave trade, from 1801 to 1807, the sugar exports of Jamaica amounted annually to an average of 133,000 hhds. During the seven years succeeding the abolition of the slave-trade, from 1807 to 1814, the annual average was 118,000 hhds.; from 1814 to 1821, 110,000 hhds.; from 1821 to 1828, 96,000 hhds.; and from 1828 to 1835, when the Emancipation Act took effect, the annual average was only 90,000 hhds. In 1859 the export was but 28,000 hhds.; but it is evident that emancipation was, at most, a remote cause of the decline. And, during all those years prior to emancipation, there was a steady diminution in the population of the island.[1]

After the Emancipation Act had passed the British Parliament, the planters, particularly in Jamaica, instead of meeting the new issues created in a fair and intelligent spirit, resolutely and

[1] Sewell, *passim.*

persistently opposed the successful working of the law. They were the legislators, and had full power to remedy and perfect the Emancipation Act. Thinking to be able to compel the freedmen to continue on their estates as before, and to labour at a price very much below the market wages, the Assembly, by an Ejectment Act, "gave to the planters the right to turn out the enfranchised peasantry, at a week's notice, from their homes; to root up their provision-grounds, and to cut down the fruit-trees. By a police-law, the ejected peasant might be arrested for trespass, if he remained an hour on the estate after due notice to quit. Compelled to purchase a freehold, the peasant was made to pay a heavy stamp-duty on the transfer and registration of the land he purchased. In slavery times, when corn was provided by the masters, the import duty was 3*d.* per barrel; for the freedman it was raised to 3*s.* On rice, salt-fish, and pork, the duty was augmented two or three hundred per cent. Driven from his cabin on his master's estate, and compelled to build a hut for himself, the customs on building materials were more than doubled, and the huts were assessed at an enormous rate. An excise duty was imposed on sugar, coffee, &c., raised by the freedmen; while the same articles raised by the planters for export were free of duty. In like manner, a costly licence to sell these articles at retail was made requisite." And a thousand other like acts of legislation, intended to oppress the peasantry, and to compel them to work for the planters on the terms imposed by the latter, were passed.[1]

But notwithstanding all these obstacles placed in the path of the negroes, they have steadily improved in their material and moral condition. The number of slaves liberated was 320,000. The mortality amongst them since has been very large, from epidemics of cholera, small-pox, &c. and from the almost utter absence of medical aid, from which cause the deaths, amongst children especially, are extremely numerous. But the diminution in the population is said to be less than it was before emancipation. Of these liberated slaves, at least 50,000 have become holders of from two to six acres of land, and tax-payers. They grow provisions for themselves and families; they supply the village markets; they raise for sale—coffee, pimento, arrowroot, fruits, and vegetables, and sometimes sugar-cane; they have their horses and other live stock, and are said to be "as

[1] See "The West Indies," by Edward Bean Underhill. London, 1862, pp. 216—221.

independent of labour for daily wages as it is possible for any peasantry to be;" many of them do devote a certain amount of time to plantation work. Published statistics show that a large trade has been gradually springing up in the products of these small farmers, which either did not exist at all prior to emancipation, or to an insignificant extent only. It is proved also that the quantity of provisions raised by these small cultivators, for domestic consumption, has been steadily increasing: thus, 194,455 barrels of provisions, besides 2,202 cwts. of bread and 83,718 bushels of corn, were imported in 1841, against 123,155 barrels of provisions, 3,024 cwt. of bread, and 20,704 bushels of corn in 1858; the diminution in the imports during the latter year having been compensated by an increased domestic production by the small farmers.[1] Mr. Sewell says, "There is indeed a vast difference between the style of living of the free peasantry of Jamaica and that of her former slaves. The people enjoy luxuries now, where they had scarce common necessaries before. The coffee, vegetables, and meat that are now indispensable to them, they never tasted before they were emancipated. A settler with an acre of land in cultivation estimates its value at £30 per annum. He grows upon it, at the same time, corn, yams, cocoas, plantains, bananas, tobacco, peas, ochra, coffee, and even sugar-cane. An acre or two will support a family of seven persons in clothes and provisions, and enable the owner to save money besides. I know settlers who have accumulated by this, and no other means, £80, and even £100, and the sum is generally devoted to the erection of improved dwellings." And this in spite of great ignorance, and poor economy in labour, which they have never been taught to remedy.

The Legislature does little or nothing to improve or educate the people. In 1859, the Assembly voted the sum of £2,950 for education, when there were 65,000 children, between the ages of five and fifteen years, upon the island.

The planters still complain that the negroes will not work. But the Chief Commissioner of Roads, who has 3,000 men in constant employment, assured Mr. Sewell that he could procure an additional thousand at any moment; the men, he said, preferred breaking stones on the road to estate-labour, though the former was much the severer work. These men work diligently five days in the week, going to market on the sixth, or devoting it to the cultivation of their own grounds. The superintendent

[1] Sewell, *op. cit.* pp. 244—259.

of the Rio Grande Copper Mines told Mr. Sewell that if he wanted five men, fifteen or twenty would apply; in his experience of eight years he has never found any difficulty in getting labourers. He says, "They work harder and more persistently, I am convinced, than if they were forced to it." And when the negro himself was asked, why he preferred the hard work of the road, or the mine, to the easier labour of an estate, he replied, "*Buckra don't pay.*" And here lies the solution of the mystery. It is the almost universal testimony that, "while labourers on the road or in the mine are paid regularly once a week, and full wages, those who work on estates often have to go two or three months without their wages; and sometimes they lose their pay altogether."[1] Of course, under these circumstances, it is no wonder that the freedmen prefer to work for themselves, or for any one who will *pay* them even moderate wages, rather than for the planters, most of whom pay in promises, or pay badly.

We have the more recent testimony as to the willingness of the blacks of Jamaica to work, of Mr. Barnes, who, in 1862, began the experiment of cotton-planting in the island. He says, "We commenced in December, 1862; and as soon as the people were told what we were going to do, thirty-two men offered themselves the first week; during the next fortnight, fifty more came; and so the number increased until, at one time, including men, women, and children, we had two hundred and thirty persons employed, of those who were said to be only fit to eat and sleep." His agent had orders to pay regularly once a week, on a given day, and always in money.

The great cheapness and economy of free-labour as compared with slave-labour is abundantly proved, by reference to the following table:—[2]

Sugar Islands.	Labour force.	Average of lbs. per man.	Annual cost of each labourer.	Cost of labour per lb. of sugar made.
Cuba	120,000	4,810	$144 30	3 cents.
Jamaica (slave)	70,000	2,286	10 00	$4\frac{37}{100}$,,
,, (free)	20,000	2,500	50 00	2 ,,
Trinidad ,, ...	17,000	3,823	66 00	$1\frac{72}{100}$,,
Barbados ,, ...	22,000	3,090	44 00	$1\frac{2}{5}$,,

[1] Sewell, *op. cit.* pp. 284, 285, 194, *et passim;* also Mr. Underhill's book.

[2] Sewell, *op. cit.* pp. 260—276. The reason why the average production per labourer is greater in Cuba is, because in Cuba the slave is made to work four or five hours longer each day than the freedmen of the other islands, and at least two days more of each week.

The present Governor of Jamaica gives the following as the result of emancipation upon the condition and prospects of the negro population of the island :—" The proportion of those who are settling themselves industriously on their own holdings, and rapidly rising in the social scale, and some of whom are, to a limited extent, themselves the employers of hired labour, which they pay for either in money or in kind, is not only steadily increasing, but is at the present moment far more extensive than was anticipated by those who are aware of all that took place in this colony in the early days of negro freedom. There can be no doubt, in fact, that an independent, respectable, and trustworthy middle class is rapidly forming. . . . Jamaica at this moment presents at once the strongest proof of the complete success of the great measure of emancipation, as relates to the capacity of the negro race for freedom, and the most unfortunate instance of a descent in the scale of agricultural and commercial importance as a colonial community." [1]

The causes of the agricultural and commercial decline, besides those to which we have alluded, are the competition which Cuba presented, under very favourable circumstances, in the production of sugar; the restrictions imposed by Great Britain upon commercial intercourse with the United States; the rapid commercial growth of the latter, whereby Jamaica lost the prominent position and advantage she once possessed as a depôt of trade between Europe and the Spanish Main, &c. &c. All these circumstances are explained by Mr. Sewell, to whose work, and to that of Mr. Underhill, as being the two most recent, we refer for much interesting information concerning the results and failings of emancipation.

The experience of the French West India Islands, so far as the progress made since emancipation is concerned, agrees with that afforded by the British Islands. An official report states that " Emancipation has impelled one portion of the slaves towards the towns, another towards the unoccupied lands, very few towards the prisons and hospitals. It has made artisans and small freeholders, some vagrants, few beggars, and few criminals." [2]

Emancipation was declared in the French colonies in 1848; the importation of coolies did not begin to effect its results until

[1] Underhill, *op. cit.* p. 438.

[2] Quoted in the " Boston Trade Report," 1863, p. 113.

after 1857. The following tables exhibit the movements of the trade of those colonies :—[1]

Islands.	Quinquennial Average of Exports and Imports.		
	1843 to 1847.	1848 to 1852.	1853 to 1857.
Martinique . . .	frs. 39,226,503	frs. 36,676,505	frs. 51,546,959
Guadaloupe . . .	39,226,912	28,641,649	39,904,671
Guiane	4,081,799	4,427,460	7,954,376
Bourbon	33,074,648	34,708,672	72,324,705
Total . . .	frs. 115,609,862	frs. 104,454,286	frs.171,730,711

This shows an average gain, in the last five years, of 56,120,849 francs over the average of the five years preceding emancipation.

In 1847, these colonies employed 2,022 vessels of all kinds in a total transportation of 115,694,170 francs of freight; in 1857, 2,488 vessels, in a transportation of 166,057,692 francs; in 1859, 3,342 vessels, in a transportation of 172,355,614 francs of freight. In exports alone the comparison stands :—

Martinique, in 1847	frs. 18,323,921	in 1857	frs. 24,830,093
Guadaloupe, ,,	20,420,522	,,	23,319,277
Guiane ,,	1,622,919	,,	961,272
Bourbon ,,	12,620,602	,,	33,130,125

Thus from all quarters—from the experience of the Southern Slave States themselves, where the experiment is being tried on a small scale as yet, and amidst all the distraction and turmoil of the war, as well as from the West India Islands—the encouragement is very great. We conceive that there can be no doubt as to the result at home, so far as the good conduct and desire to improve of the negro are concerned; for the slaves of our Southern States are farther removed from pure African than were those of the West Indies at the time of the emancipation, the slave-trade having been longer abolished with us; and we believe, too, that our negroes have been treated, on the whole, with more mildness, and that they are more intelligent, docile, and educable. Moreover, the military training, which so many of them are receiving, will temper and perfect the education which they have acquired in the school of expectancy, in which they seem to have been awaiting their freedom.

We believe, also, that the whites will receive and adapt themselves to the new order of things with more willingness than

[1] Quoted in the "Boston Trade Report," p. 112.

did the planters of the West Indies. The rapidity of the progress of emancipation in the Border States, and the comparative alacrity with which it has been received even in Louisiana and Arkansas, warrant us in indulging that belief. Capital, and energy, and goodwill will not be wanting, as they were in the British islands, to favour the success of the experiment. If the original planters of the South should fail, either from pride or from ignorance, hundreds of Northern farmers will take their places, as, indeed, they are already doing, and will bring wealth, zeal, enterprise, and skill to aid in regenerating the country. And among the mass of the Southern people who have never been slave-holders, but who have been kept depressed and impoverished by slavery, will gradually spring up a knowledge of their own interests and a desire to secure them, which will complete the great work, and place the Union upon a better and a more solid basis than it has ever had before.

"Slavery once overthrown," says an eloquent and accomplished French writer in the *Revue des Deux Mondes*, "the field will be left open to the operation of that spirit of enterprise which has made the New England States so justly admired by the friends of civilization. Then will the Tree of Liberty produce abundantly its fruits; and the world will see what a Republic truly democratic can accomplish in science, in art, and in social economy, when it shall be once fairly engaged in the elaboration of all sorts of improvements, with that persevering energy which characterizes the American mind. What Liberty has already accomplished in the New England States, it will secure, we doubt not, throughout all that vast Anglo-Saxon Republic, when the crime of slavery shall have been expiated, and when the slave, freed from his chains, shall grasp as a friend's the hand of his former master."

We believe that the great mass of the English people would hail with joy this glorious consummation. We are persuaded that the true interests of England would be immeasurably advanced by such a regeneration of the great American Union; *not* by an illusory promise of free-trade with an independent "Slave Republic," nor by a political alliance, at once illusory and disgraceful.